# My Jesus, My Hero

Lilly Simon

ISBN 978-1-63814-038-2 (Paperback)
ISBN 978-1-63814-039-9 (Digital)

Covenant Books
11661 Hwy 707
Murrells Inlet, SC 29576
www.covenantbooks.com

To all the people in the world. May you experience the outpouring love of Jesus.

# Introduction

*For God so loved the world that he gave his only Son, so that everyone who believes in him might not perish but might have eternal life.*
—John 3:16 (NABRE)

God has always loved us as His precious children. We were always supposed to be in communion with the Lord, our Father, and have eternal life, but this was lost when sin entered the world through Adam and Eve's disobedience and distrust of God. Through many prophets, God tried to bring humanity back to His love, but the people remained far from it. Finally, God sent his only son Jesus Christ to save us and bring us back to the Father's love.

Psalm 136:1–9 (NABRE) tells us:

> Praise the LORD, for he is good; for his mercy endures forever; Praise the God of gods; for his mercy endures forever; Praise the Lord of lords; for his mercy endures forever; Who alone has done great wonders, for his mercy endures forever; Who skillfully made the heavens, for his mercy endures forever; Who spread the earth upon the waters, for his mercy endures forever; Who made the great lights, for his mercy endures forever; The sun to rule the day, for his mercy endures forever; The moon and stars to rule the night, for his mercy endures forever.

Yes, Lord, I hope to share your mercy, love, and what you have done for me and my family to others; your mercy endures forever.

My name is Lillykutty Simon, and I invite you to come on a journey with me as I share my story. I felt inspired to put pen to paper to share about the goodness of God. Whatever you might be going through, my hope is you experience love. Most of us have heard the phrase "God loves you," so you may know that I am married to my husband, Johney, and we have four children: Noel, Nancy, Navya, and Nova, who is in heaven. I was born in a small village called Manjamattam, located in Kottayam district, Kerala, India.

I am the fourteenth child of my father and the eighth child of my mother. Allow me to clarify—my father, Ouseph, and my mother, Kathreena, were both married and widowed before they married each other. Both of their first spouses passed away young. My father's first wife passed away after they had seven children, and my mom's first husband passed away after they had one child. May God rest their souls. After a few years, my father and mother got married. They had eight children together. In that, I am the seventh child. All together, we were sixteen children. We never considered separation; rather, we lived as one big family. My father and mother were God-fearing people.

I never thought I would write a book; I know this happened thanks to God's providence. If it were not for the Holy Spirit's inspiration and Jesus giving me a title for the book, I would not have written this book.

This journey began in 2015 when I was diagnosed with breast cancer. When I was resting at home after cancer surgery, our parish vicar, Fr. Ligory, visited me, as it's the custom for a parish priest to visit sick parishioners. He was very concerned about my faith because people sometimes tend to fall away from their faith when they experience illness or hardship. They start to question whether or not God exists. I have heard the question "WHY ME?" very often. However, by God's grace, I never had to ask that question because I knew why it had to happen.

Ephesians 2:10 (NABRE) states, "For we are his handiwork, created in Christ Jesus for the good works that God has prepared in advance, that we should live in them." I knew from the beginning of my cancer diagnosis and treatment that JESUS has a plan for me, as Jeremiah 29:11 (RSVCE) states: "For I know the plans I have for you, says the LORD, plans for welfare and not for evil, to give you a future and a hope."

While we were talking about my cancer, Fr. Ligory realized that my faith became deeper than before. He was very happy that my faith was increasing in the midst of physical suffering. Then I shared with him my past encounters with Jesus and how Jesus healed me and raised me as a witness while attending a live charismatic retreat online. Then with a smile on his face, Fr. Ligory encouraged my daughter, Navya, to make sure I write down all these true stories of the goodness of God in a book. We laughed it off; I did not take it seriously.

Then in July 2016, my husband, me, and a couple of our family friends, together we drove to Washington to attend a stay-in charismatic retreat. It was from July 14 to 17, and we stayed in the hotel where the retreat was conducted. On Saturday, July 16, 2016, during the Holy Mass, this word came into my heart, "My Jesus, My Hero." As soon as the Holy Mass was over, I wrote these words down in my notebook. Later in the day, I shared these words with a priest whom I met at the retreat and told him about my journey with cancer.

The priest confirmed to me that these words were to be the title of my book. So I began thinking and praying about recording my cancer journey and my personal encounter with Jesus. The whole year passed by and nothing happened, and I forgot to write it in the book. But on February 16, 2017, during Eucharistic adoration in my local Catholic church, I received inspiration to start writing.

I wrote down some of the events that happened in my life. But then again, I completely forgot and did not write until 2020 when COVID-19 arrived on the scene. I heard in the news how people were expressing their feeling toward doctors and nurses and other people, too, calling them their HEROES. Then in my heart, a strong feeling arose. I felt the HOLY SPIRIT talking to me about Jesus who died for me. Only a superhero can do supernatural things, and I was thinking how amazing it is that Jesus loved us so much He was willing to die on a cross and sacrifice His life in order to save all humanity from sin.

Jesus only did good things to everyone, but the people of His times did not see it this way. Pilate knew Jesus was handed over because of the jealousy of the chief priests, as it was written: "For he knew that it was out of envy that the chief priests had handed him over" (Mark 15:10 NABRE). Because of the chief priests' jealousy, they killed Jesus (Mark 15:10), and they did not recognize Jesus who is the SON of the living GOD. Then I started to think more about Jesus and started to read the Bible. While I was reading the Bible, the Word of GOD came to my mind and heart and started to talk to me about how much God loves each one of us and how HIS mercy endures forever. I learned that we all are GOD's children and GOD IS OUR HEAVENLY FATHER. Even though we do not love GOD as much as we are supposed to, even if we do not love him at all, HE is patiently waiting for our return to him with all our heart and mind. The first commandment JESUS teaches us is to *LOVE GOD WHOLEHEARTEDLY.*

Many times, we abandon GOD due to our pride or our ignorance about GOD's MERCY. The parable of the Prodigal Son in Luke 15:11–32 is a perfect example of this. Just as the father in the story, our heavenly Father patiently awaits our complete return from sin because without holiness, we cannot enter the kingdom of heaven. In order to get into heaven, the first thing we must do is to trust Jesus completely and believe that he is the only son of the FATHER IN HEAVEN. Secondly, we must repent of our sins; in the beginning of Jesus's public ministry, he teaches us this: "After John had been arrested, Jesus came to Galilee proclaiming the gospel of God: This is the time of fulfillment. The kingdom of God is at hand. Repent, and believe in the gospel" (Mark 1:14–15 NABRE). It is also stated in Saint Paul's letter to the Romans 5:8 (GNT), "But GOD has shown us how much he loves us—it was while we were still sinners that Christ died for us!" That's the truth, JESUS willingly died on the cross for the sins of all mankind—those living, those dead, and those yet to be born until the end of the world.

Some people asked me, what is my goal in writing this book? My mission is to reach out to all the people in the world about God's mercy and love and about how much Jesus is sad when people do not love God and one another. Jesus is GOD, and he made heaven, earth, and everything in it. He gave the men freedom to choose good and bad, and it's our responsibility to choose good and hate evil things. The sadness of Jesus's heart is shared with Saint Bridget of Sweden, who was a mystic and saint and the founder of the Bridgettines nuns and monks after the death of her husband of twenty years.

She loved Jesus very much and wanted to know about the number of blows OUR LORD JESUS received during HIS passion. One day, while she was meditating on Jesus's passion, Jesus appeared to her and told her about the details of HIS passion. He taught the fifteen prayers on the passion of JESUS CHRIST and also told her that many people are not believing in his sacred passion and are staying in the state of sin and wanting nothing to do with Jesus's mercy, giving their life to the devil and finally going to the eternal fire. So when I read these special prayers and Jesus's vision to Saint Bridget, I felt the sadness of Jesus in my heart.

A desire began to unfold within me: *How can I help others to know the Lord?* I remember in the past when I prayed with a spiritual counselor. He shared with me *that Jesus says,* "I thirst." At that time, I didn't really know what this meant, and I forgot about it shortly after. After being diagnosed with cancer, looking back to that prayer experience, I believe Jesus was calling me to help save souls through intercessory prayer. I realized Jesus's mercy and love for me when I got cancer, and that was the start of something new.

A couple of years ago, I heard about many young adults dying from overdosing on drugs, and this made me very sad. I started to pray for all children, especially those with addictions. This inspired the formation of an intercession group of mothers, where we pray for all people in all different kinds of situations: the sick, dying, incarcerated, and all the other people in the world. When the Holy Spirit comes into us, we are inspired to do the right thing. And we will be led away from immoral actions including drugs, alcohol, premarital sex, abortion, adultery, prostitution, homosexual behaviors, and so forth. God created us for love, and sin distorts the goodness God wants for us. Sometimes we make bad choices, but that does not make us a bad person—God's mercy is always available to us, and encountering His mercy makes us new. Praying to the Holy Spirit for wisdom will help us in making good choices and not fall into sin. In 1 Corinthians 6:19–20 (NABRE), it says, "Do you not know that your body is a temple of the holy Spirit within you, whom you have from God, and that you are not your own? For you have been purchased at a price. Therefore, glorify God in your body." Let us love and respect ourselves and others—in word and deed—with the help of the Holy Spirit.

My goal is to share how God has worked in my life and to encourage all of you, especially those who are suffering, to invite God into your life and experience Jesus transforming your suffering into something beautiful.

I desire this transformation for all people, especially those who are suffering from terminal illness, those who have lost hope, those who are oppressed, and those who have no one to take care of their body or soul. I wish this for those who are incarcerated, whether innocent or guilty, and those who have not had a personal encounter with Jesus. I also desire for all Christians to come to encounter the real presence of Jesus in the Eucharist. My goal is to share the love I have experienced from Jesus throughout my life. I hope this will inspire my readers to have a personal encounter with Jesus. Why? Because Jesus loves each one of us personally and uniquely. I also want to reach the people who do not know about Jesus's unfathomable love and mercy that he has for each and every one of us. I hope and pray that one day you all, my dearest readers, will also be able to have your own experiences filled with the love of Jesus.

Jesus works with each person in different ways. Jesus's love is unique and present with all of us even if we do not feel it at the time. It does not matter who you are; even if you do not know Jesus, He knows you personally and is with you at the door of your heart, knocking.

> You formed my inmost being; you knit me in my mother's womb. I praise you, because I am wonderfully made; wonderful are your works! My very self you know. My bones are not hidden from you, When I was being made in secret, fash-

ioned in the depths of the earth. (Psalm 139:13–
15 NABRE)

Yes, Lord, it is absolutely true that you formed me in my mother's womb. I know that you chose me to bear fruit.

In the Gospel of Saint John 15:1–5 (NABRE), Jesus tells us,

> I am the true vine, and my Father is the vine
> grower. He takes away every branch in me that
> does not bear fruit, and every one that does he
> prunes so that it bears more fruit. You are already
> pruned because of the word that I spoke to you.
> Remain in me, as I remain in you. Just as a branch
> cannot bear fruit on its own unless it remains on
> the vine, so neither can you unless you remain in
> me. I am the vine; you are the branches. Whoever
> remains in me and I in him will bear much fruit,
> because without me you can do nothing.

Jesus is the vine, and we are the branches. Everyone in this world
is God's child, whether you are an infant, a teenager, a young adult,
middle-aged, or an elderly. We all are God's children, his precious son
or daughter. Your nationality, your economic status, your profession,
the size of your bank account, whether you have a home—none of
this defines you. Nobody can strip you of your dignity, the fact that
you are a precious child of God. As the branches are close to the vine,
likewise we ought to stay close to God. In the Gospel of Saint John
15:10 (NABRE) says, "If you keep my commandments, you will
remain in my love, just as I have kept my Father's commandments
and remain in his love."

The heavenly Father's will is to save mankind from their sins
after Adam and Eve disobeyed GOD and lost paradise; he desired to
bring all his children back to the heavenly kingdom. We read in the
Old Testament how God the Father sent out his prophets to rescue
the Israelites from Egyptian slavery. However, once they got their
freedom, they again started to sin against GOD and disobey his com-

mandments. But GOD the Father was very patient and merciful to his own children, the Israelites, and in order to save them from their sins, the prophets instructed them to obey GOD's commandments and love GOD and their neighbors, but they hardened their hearts and disobeyed the prophets.

I see a likeness between the Israelites and the people in this generation; they continue to disobey GOD's commandments and do not love GOD from their hearts. We see that in our world, people do not love one another as Christ loved—selflessly and sacrificially. People kill each other, steal, destroy, rape, abort, have envy, anger, lie, etc. We are seeing more evil things in this world in our present time. What can we do to prevent all these things? I see only one solution, and that is to come back to GOD and believe in JESUS. Trust in Jesus and love Jesus with all your heart and mind and love your neighbor as yourself. If people die in their sins, they will lose their eternal life and go to eternal damnation. That is the reason GOD the Father sent his only SON Jesus to the world for their salvation.

> The people who sit in darkness have seen a
> great light, on those dwelling in a land overshad-
> owed by death light has arisen. (Matthew 4:16
> NABRE)

That light is JESUS. I am writing about the same Jesus who was born 2,023 years ago, lived only thirty-three years, walked in the streets of Jerusalem and neighboring places, obeyed his Father's command, bore our sins, and carried his cross. Jesus obeyed his Father until death. Jesus bore the sins of all humankind when he willingly accepted the cross. In 740 to 700 BC, the prophet Isaiah prophesied about the birth of JESUS AND HIS DEATH. See Isaiah 7:14, 9:6–7 and all of Isaiah chapter 53. These passages are referenced by Saint Paul in his letter to the Philippians in chapter 2, verses 1 to 11.

The entire BIBLE is worth reading; it gives us wisdom from heaven. It is a gift from God the Father and shows how much he loves each one of us. It gives us guidance on how we should live from birth to death. The Acts of the Apostles gives a clear picture of the risen Jesus and how Jesus helped the disciples to proclaim the gospel by bestowing upon them the gift of the Holy SPIRIT. When the apostles proclaimed Jesus's name, the sick were healed and the dead were raised to life. Also, ACTS 9:1–31 shares about the conversion of Paul from being a killer of Christians to being one of the most zealous preachers of Christ. THESE are not just stories. Everything written in the Bible is the truth about the whole life of Jesus and His apostles.

So when you look at Saint Paul's life, every sinner can become a saint. That is Jesus's ultimate wish, for a sinner to repent, and Jesus teaches us that when one sinner repents, heaven rejoices the most. Jesus teaches us the story of the lost sheep where the good shepherd, who had one hundred sheep, found out that one got lost. Then he left the ninety-nine and went after the one lost sheep. And when he found the lost sheep, he put that sheep on his shoulder and was very happy. That is what Jesus said to the Pharisees in the Gospel of Saint Matthew chapter 9, verse 13, that he came to call the sinners, not the righteous. The "lost sheep" story can be found in the Gospel of Saint Luke chapter 15, verses 1 to 7.

I see myself as a poor sinner whom Jesus loves. He called me by name after healing me from my cancer and asked me to write my experiences and personal encounter with him, who is the son of the Almighty GOD, as Saint Paul says in the Acts 9:20 (NABRE), "And he began at once to proclaim Jesus in the synagogues, that he is the Son of God." That same Jesus is still alive and giving visions to many of his children. I will also be writing about Saint Faustina, a Polish nun to whom JESUS APPEARED many times, and asked her to write about JESUS'S MERCY AND LOVE to all mankind. He taught her THE DIVINE MERCY CHAPLET. She was called Jesus's secretary of Divine Mercy. Jesus is waiting for me and you and is teaching us to come back to him and leave all our sinful ways of life. Even to this day, Jesus is catching many people like me. Jesus is the only TRUE GOD who made heaven, earth, and everything in it.

Jesus teaches us the most important things in life in the Gospel of Saint Luke 10:25–37 (NABRE).

> There was a scholar of the law who stood up to test him and said, "Teacher, what must I do to inherit eternal life?" Jesus said to him, "What is written in the law? How do you read it?" He said in reply, "You shall love the Lord, your God, with all your heart, with all your being, with all your strength, and with all your mind, and your neighbor as yourself." He replied to him, "You have answered correctly; do this and you will live." But because he wished to justify himself, he said to Jesus, "And who is my neighbor?" Jesus replied, "A man fell victim to robbers as he went down from Jerusalem to Jericho. They stripped and beat him and went off leaving him half-dead. A priest happened to be going down that road, but when he saw him, he passed by on the opposite side. Likewise, a Levite came to the place, and when he saw him, he passed by on the opposite side. But a Samaritan traveler who came upon him was moved with compassion at the sight. He approached the victim, poured oil and wine over his wounds and bandaged them. Then he lifted him up on his own animal, took him to an inn and cared for him. The next day he took out two silver coins and gave them to the innkeeper with the instruction, 'Take care of him. If you spend more than what I have given you, I shall repay you on my way back.' Which of these three, in your opinion, was a neighbor to the robbers' victim?" He answered, "The one who treated him with mercy." Jesus said to him, "Go and do likewise."

There you have it, your neighbor is whoever you have contact with every single day of your life—a coworker, teacher, grocery store worker, sanitation worker, bus driver, doctor, homeless person, friend, or family member, etc. Jesus is asking each one of us to be humble, merciful, and loving to our *neighbor* daily. When you love one another, you would not do wrong to them. When you think of your best friend, you would think about how you can make them happy. You would never want to hurt that person. As Christians, we believe every person is created by God and is God's child. We also believe that God lives within every single person.

Jesus is love.

> Beloved, let us love one another, because love is of God; everyone who loves is begotten by God and knows God. Whoever is without love does not know God, for God is love. In this way the love of God was revealed to us: God sent his only Son into the world so that we might have life through him. In this is love: not that we have loved God, but that he loved us and sent his Son for the forgiveness of our sins. Beloved, if God so loved us, we also must love one another. No one has ever seen God. Yet, if we love one another, God remains in us, and his love is brought to perfection in us. This is how we know that we remain in him and he in us, that he has given us of his Spirit. Moreover, we have seen and testified that the Father sent his Son as a savior of the world. Whoever acknowledges that Jesus is the Son of God, God remains in him and he in God. We have come to know and to believe in the love God has for us. God is love, and whoever remains in love remains in God and God in him. In this, love is brought to perfection among us, that we have confidence on the day of judgment because as he is, so are we in this world. There is no fear

in love, but perfect love drives out fear because fear has to do with punishment, and so one who fears is not yet perfect in love. We love because he first loved us. If anyone says, "I love God," but hates his brother, he is a liar; for whoever does not love a brother whom he has seen cannot love God, whom he has not seen. This is the commandment we have from him: whoever loves God must also love his brother. (1 John 4:7–21 NABRE)

My dear brothers and sisters, I want to convey how the Lord has loved, called, and talked to me personally and given me the courage to tell the world that he is *my Jesus, my hero.*

The information in this memoir is from various sources, including my mom, brothers, sisters, sisters-in-law, and tells of my own experiences from my life as a daughter, sister, wife, mother, nurse, and also a cancer survivor, as well as how I got the personal encounter with Jesus and how Jesus raised me as a witness and to be His disciple. All the details will be revealed in later chapters!

# Chapter 1

## CHILDHOOD

My father was born in Manjamattam, and my mother was born in a small village called Punnathura, Kerala. She was the eldest out of eight children. Her father passed away at a young age, and she was raised by her mother. She was married at a young age, and when she was twenty-two, she had her first child. Her husband passed away when the baby was only three years old.

After my parents (whom I called Chachan and Ammachi) had both become widowed, Ammachi's maternal aunt, who had been living in Chachan's hometown, suggested Chachan and Ammachi's union. They got married in 1951 and had eight children together. Altogether we are sixteen children, and I am number fifteen. As Psalms 127:3 (GNT) says, "children are a gift from the Lord, they are a real blessing." Couples in that generation knew that all the children are the gift from our heavenly Father. In our village, many of our neighbors had at least five children, sometimes ten or more. The number of children in the family was not dependent on income; in everything, the families depended on God, who created them.

A village called Manjamattam, with little streams, small rivers, and a few hills, is where I was born and brought up. My father and mother were God-fearing people. In the morning, I used to wake up to the sound of my father's morning prayer of reciting the Psalms, starting at 4:00 a.m., but I always went back to sleep until my mom would call me to get ready for school. My father, after his morning

1

prayers, would take part in our local parish's 6:00 a.m. Holy Mass. At this time, my mom used to be very busy cooking food for the family.

In Manjamattam, the small village, there were only about 250 families. We all knew one another, and we had a close relationship with our neighbors. I used to play with the children in the yard and go down to the river, which was in front of our house in a valley. When we were children, this is where we would take a bath. My friends and I would catch fish with a towel. Sometimes we would throw the fish back, and sometimes we would bring the fish home and put it in a bottle of water and keep them. We would walk to school with friends and on some weekdays go to church.

My school years were so memorable! I studied in the convent school near our local parish. The main thing I remember is, if it were not raining, we would be learning outdoors, under a tree. We would all sit in the grass around our teacher, who would sit on a chair. Extracurricular activities, especially sports, were encouraged. I still remember playing on the school grounds with my friends. Lunchtime was fun as well because my friends and I would exchange lunch portions, and thus, we would have a feast! I also remember that we were always going to church just to pray, especially during exam time. We did not pray very hard because we knew we could rely on the nuns in the convent to pray for us! In reality, I did not know how to pray.

When I grew up in the village, no one spoke or heard about ABORTION. Now it's a common word everywhere in the world. We are killing babies whom God created, and the cry of innocent babies has reached the throne of God. We must repent to God and do reparation for abortion in the world. (I posted a special prayer for all the innocent victims of abortion. Jesus promised Barnabas Nwoye, a visionary from Nigeria, special blessings to whoever recites this prayer and teaches others.)

Prayer for the Baptism of Aborted Babies

Heavenly Father, Your love is eternal. In
Your ocean of love, You saved the world through

Your only-begotten Son, Jesus Christ. Now look at Your only Son on the Cross Who is constantly bleeding for love of His people, and forgive Your world. Purify and baptize aborted children with the Precious Blood and Water from the Sacred Side of Your Son, Who hung dead on the Cross for their salvation, in the Name of the Father, and of the Son, and of the Holy Spirit. May they, through the Holy Death of Jesus Christ gain everlasting life, through His Wounds be healed, and through His Precious Blood be freed. There to rejoice with the Saints in Heaven. Amen.

This prayer is found *in Devotion to the Most Precious Blood of Our Lord Jesus Christ.* The people were GOD-fearing where I grew up. My father would always tell us, "God will provide." We were a middle-class family, and my father was well respected as a God-fearing and honest man.

In 1964, my father's honesty was proven when one of his friends—a rich man—gave him stewardship of his property and house for two years. We enjoyed the land, house, and all the fruits and vegetables while my father took care of the property. Although we were a middle-class family, my father was well respected; he was a God-fearing and honest man. My Chachan's closest friend's name was Kuriakose. We lovingly called him Kuriakose Chettan. He trusted my Chachan very much so—the most in the neighborhood. They were neighbors growing up. Kuriakose Chettan was a very wealthy man from his family heritage yet also humble and noble. My Chachan and Kuriakose Chettan had an *alma bendham*, meaning "soul connection."

Kuriakose Chettan moved to another town and left behind ten acres of land with a large house. It was a twenty-minute walk from our old home. Kuriakose Chettan allowed our family to stay in their large house for free. My eldest sister remembers carrying me there as our family moved into this rich family's house. This estate was surrounded by all kinds of fruits and vegetables: oranges, lemons, bananas, guava, *chambanga* (rose apple), mango, jackfruit, papaya, and tender coconut. After two years, we went back to our old house, for it was only for this time that Kuriakose Chettan needed us there.

In Kerala, most households had a farm of livestock, vegetables, and spices. My father was a merchant. He used to buy rubber goods and spices, including black pepper, ginger, dry ginger, turmeric, among others, and go to the trading centers in various towns such as Alappuzha, Kottayam, and Pala to trade goods and make a living for our family. Chachan would travel by way of a bullock wagon with his goods and driver.

One day in 1963, when I was in my mother's womb, my father was traveling on the dirt roads to work when the driver veered to the side of the road for an oncoming pickup truck to pass. Chachan, who had not heeded the warning of the driver to sit in a safer position in the cart, got flung into the road, fracturing his shoulder and hand. When I grew up, my mom told me that it was the local buzz that Chachan walked away with only minor injuries because of the blessings I had brought to the family at my birth. The protection God gave my dad was incredible.

When we are under the wings of the Almighty God, the Creator of this world, even if we were to meet with an accident or unforeseen adversity, we only need to trust in the Lord. Without his knowledge, nothing will happen in our life or in this world. Let us pray for the security of God's protection daily as written in Psalm 91.

I remember seeing a powerful testimony by an intensive care doctor on CNN. She spoke of surviving the coronavirus by reciting Psalm 91. For those who do not know about PSALM 91, it's in the BIBLE. The WORD OF GOD never fails. The Word of God is Jesus, and he is alive, only we must have the faith in him to see the glory of GOD.

Kerala is home to many religions. I belong to the Syro-Malabar rite, an eastern rite of the Catholic Church. Every town has at least one Catholic church. Saint Sebastian Syro-Malabar Catholic Church was my home parish. At seven o'clock every night, the church bells would ring, and that meant it was time for evening prayer with the family. At that time, my family, along with all our Catholic neighbors, would pray the Rosary in our homes. Some days my father would come home late, but when he heard the church bells, he would stop, kneel, and pray.

Once, when my father was walking home after work, he happened to be in front of a Hindu family's home when he heard the church bell at 7:00 p.m. Right away, my father knelt and started to pray. The matron of the household asked my father what he was doing, and my father testified to the love of Christ to her, a person who did not believe in Jesus Christ, the true and living GOD. My father always gave witness to Jesus wherever he was. I am certain that all the blessings I received are because of my father's strong faith. My older sister, Chinnamma Chechy, told me the story of how one time, during Eucharistic Adoration in my home parish, my father saw a light emanating from the Blessed Sacrament and piercing his heart. That encounter helped him to deepen his faith in Jesus. He always gave Jesus the first place in his life. It also helped me to become who I am today.

Chachan (my dad) used to go to work every day except Sundays until he was about seventy years old. He was a very hardworking man. He never went to the theater to see movies. He always depended on GOD's providence and taught everyone, including his children, by his own example, the importance of depending on GOD's providence. I have never seen my father angry, except one time when my brother was caught smoking a cigarette.

My mother also was very hardworking. She was a housewife. She told me that she helped her mother starting at the age of four by handing her utensils while cooking. With humble beginnings, she matured into an amazing cook. After Ammachi became the new bride of my father and moved to Manjamattam, she was well known for her cooking, especially her beef curry and fish curry. Even my children will say Ammachi's beef curry is so tasty.

In fact, our neighbors and relatives would call Ammachi to be the main cook for wedding receptions, which occurred in the house of the groom. They would put a big tent in front of the house for the guests to sit in and enjoy lunch. Most of the wedding was in the morning, and the reception would usually be in the afternoon.

My Ammachi would willingly and freely give of her time and talent. Ammachi used to tell me, "Do not ask anyone for anything, just give if you can." She taught us to be happy with what we have been blessed with.

Ammachi's prayer was her household work. In those days, most women were housewives, and they spent their days taking care of children and doing the household chores. Ammachi would also wake up every day at 4:00 a.m. and start doing her chores. She would offer all her work to God and she loved her family. She cared for her stepchildren as her own. Whenever she would make special dishes, she would send me and my baby sister, Reji, to give some to our neighbors.

They were mostly Hindus, and Ammachi would share Jesus's love through her cooking. In her later years, Ammachi would spend time in personal prayer, reading spiritual books, and helping with the cooking. When she experienced bodily pain in the knee or legs, she would make the sign of the cross on that body part and exclaim, "My Jesus, heal me!" Ammachi always depended on God. The good Lord has blessed me with the same mindset as my mother.

As I mentioned earlier, my siblings and I would wake up hearing my father singing aloud his prayers at 4:00 a.m. each day. I vividly remember two specific prayers: "Please allow my wandering son to return home" (my half brother had run away when he was thirteen years old) and "Allow me to die on a first Saturday."

My father had a special devotion to our Blessed Mother. My father used to go to confession and receive Holy Communion every first Saturday of the month. He also used to wear the brown scapular to honor our Blessed Mother. It is through our faith that our Blessed Mother revealed to Sr. Lucia that she would be present at the hour of death when we have these devotions. I have adopted these devotions for myself. Not understanding why my father was praying this way, I once asked him when I was a young teenager, "Why are you praying like that?"

He replied, "Your older half brother Chacko left home many years ago, and nobody knows where he is. He left home before you were even born!" I was surprised! He had run away from home because my father scolded him for smoking, gambling, and skipping school.

By God's grace, a few years later, we received a letter from him telling us that he was coming back home. We were so excited, especially Chachan. A few members of my family went to receive him at the railway station. He brought so many things for us—new clothes, wool blankets, and lots of money. He had been living and working in Delhi. He was very generous and had a good heart. He paid for the renovation of our humble two-bedroom house. My brother Chacko (we affectionately call him Kako Kunjagala) loved me and my baby sister Regi a lot. He showed care and compassion toward everyone, but especially toward us since we were the youngest in the house. My beloved Kako Kunjagala passed away in June 2010. May his soul rest in peace.

When I was a little girl, I would tag along with Chachan to go to church. Chachan's schedule looked like this: wake up at 4:00 a.m. to pray and sing Psalms, attend the 6:00 a.m. Holy Mass, and then either stop at *Swamy's local breakfast shop*, which was well known for dosha (a kind of pancake) and coconut chutney, or come home for breakfast. Then he would go to work and return home in the evening.

Ammachi reminded me of these stories. I would hold my dad's hand and walk to church with him. Ammachi would say, "Lillykutty (everyone called me Lillykutty at home) is going to church with Chachan to eat Dosha from Swamy's shop." I still remember how soft those doshas were and the perfectly made coconut chutney. Those were the times in which I was ignorant of what the Holy Mass was or why we went to church.

In Catholic churches all around the world, twelve men are chosen to have their feet washed every year on Holy Thursday. This tradition has continued for over two thousand years in remembrance of what Jesus did for his disciples on the day before his passion and death. Jesus washed his disciples' feet and, thus, showed them that they must also be humble like him and serve their disciples.

One year, I went to church with my father on Holy Thursday. My father was one of the twelve people who had been chosen from our parish to get their feet washed by the priest. Since I was only four or five years old, I sat near my dad, so we were a total of thirteen people. I do not remember the story, but my mom told me that everyone at the church was amused. Even the nuns in the convent joked about it, saying, "This year, Jesus had thirteen apostles!" When I think of this incident now, it makes me so happy that Jesus chose me as his own a long time ago. At that age, I did not know much about Jesus or his disciples. But when the time came, Jesus called me as a witness to testify about him and proclaim that Jesus is our only Lord and Savior.

I still remember going to Christmas Mass every year at midnight and falling asleep, as I usually did, and the elderly women looking at me with pity.

Loving almighty Jesus, even though I did not love you, I thank you for having always loved me and for your everlasting mercy.

# Chapter 2

## SCHOOL YEARS

Saint Joseph's Girls School, which is a convent school run by nuns, is where I studied from first grade to tenth grade. I used to walk to school with my friends; life was very simple in those times. Usually, during the hottest part of the summer, the wells in most homes would dry up. Our family's well, which was right behind our house, very seldom dried up. Therefore, so many of our neighbors would come to my home to draw water. Ammachi was very generous to give water freely to our neighbors.

Behind the well in our backyard was a twelve-foot wall made of mud. One day, Reji, my younger sister, and I went to pick up some vegetables from our yard. We were walking single file, with me leading. It was a very narrow path with only enough space for one person to walk. The previous night had been very rainy, and when the mud was wet, there was a chance for it to break apart and you could fall off this mud ledge. I told my sister, "Reji, walk slowly and carefully, there is wet mud here. See to it that you don't fall!"

As soon as I confidently told her as a big sister would, I suddenly slipped and fell off the tall mud ledge. In between that wall of mud and the well was a little space of about one and a half feet, filled with small and big rocks. That is where I landed, just behind the well. This well had no covering of any sort; it was completely open to the twenty-one-foot-deep waters. However, my Lord Jesus protected me during that fall, and I escaped without a scratch. At that time, I did not know Psalm 91. Now I realize how powerful Jesus's protection is and how much he cared for me and continues to do so throughout my life.

Jesus, the Almighty GOD, protects each one of you just as he protected me. There was another incident in my life in which I felt God's protection. I had just finished giving my three-year-old daughter a bath, and she was standing on top of the closed toilet bowl, ready for me to towel-dry her. I was playing with her while drying her and I stretched out both my hands to pick her up. Suddenly, she jumped onto me. I was not steady to catch her, and so I fell with her on top of me into the bathtub. My knees interfaced with the tub ledge, and my body remained suspended in that position. My head did not hit the back wall, and my back did not slam onto the floor of the tub. I realized that my Jesus had sent the angels to protect me during that fall, which is why I again escaped without any injury.

These two incidents could have left me paralyzed. My Jesus, with how much care you protected me, I did not know that you were with me then, but I now realize that you were with me all along.

Ammachi loved to see us children dancing with beautiful dresses and, therefore, sent Regi and me for folk dance lessons for a couple of years when I was in middle school. My older sister, Kunju Mary Chechy, had been helping me get ready for my school's anniversary performance, and I heard my friends calling me from the road. I became very excited and was beginning to run outside when Kunju Mary Chechy said, "Lilly, let me put one more slide in your hair!"

I kept running in excitement. I jumped off from the porch and ran to the steps while trying to make it down to the road. My home was elevated, and there were eighteen stone steps leading up to my home from the road. I slipped on the first step, tumbled down the stairs, and landed at the very bottom, breaking the fall with my forehead. Ammachi ran to me and spanked me for being careless. I was not allowed to participate in the performance that day, so I stayed home and took a rest. I still have the mark on my forehead.

Another memory from middle school is when I took a field trip to see Indira Gandhi, the first woman Prime Minister of India, who visited Pala, a town in Kerala, for the *Lakshum Pushpa mela* event. One hundred thousand children from all over Kerala came to see her and hear her speech. I was there with my classmates, and we were walking in a long line to see her up close. Suddenly, I got pushed into a stone pillar and had blood gushing down my face. I still have this mark as well. Whenever I remember these incidents, I am reminded of how God's protection has been with me throughout my life.

The reason I am writing these things is to let you know that Jesus has a plan for each one of us. To achieve that plan, we need to receive GOD's wisdom. Wisdom 9:17–18 (GNT) teaches us, "No one has ever learned your will, unless you first gave him wisdom, and sent your holy spirit down to him. In this way people on earth have been set on the right path, have learned what pleases you, and have been kept safe by wisdom." Thus, we can pray to God to obtain the Holy Spirit, who teaches us everything in life, and to get wisdom from GOD. The Holy Spirit can help us with physical and spiritual things. I have had many occasions where, when I was cooking, I sometimes added more ingredients and made the curry taste bad. One time, when I was making beef curry, it turned out sour. Then I prayed and was inspired to add one cup of water, and when my husband tasted it, my husband said it was very good. Many times the Holy Spirit helped me to be a better cook. I acknowledge and thank the Holy Spirit for His wisdom that He poured on me, even in material things. The Holy Spirit will help us become the disciple of Jesus if we wanted to.

During this time, I had pets: cats, a dog, and four goats, including two baby goats. One day, one of the baby goats ate a tapioca leaf, and this had a poisonous effect on her. I gave her the herbal home remedies that my neighbor had suggested and spent that whole night with my baby goat in her barn. In the morning, my pet was healed. This made me realize how God takes care of everything in the world because he created the universe and everything in it.

During my high school years, a blind man would pass by in front of our house every summer. We knew he was blind because he walked with a stick and would also ring a bell. When Chachan (MY DAD) would hear the bell, he would tell me to go down to the road and bring him to our home. Obeying Chachan's orders, I would wait at the bottom step for this man, hold his hand, lead him up the eighteen steps, wash his feet, give him food, and allow him to rest awhile before leaving. Another memory I have of my father's caring nature for the poor is when Chachan allowed a beggar to sleep in the house. My parents' generosity toward the poor and needy molded my heart. They loved Jesus and loved the poor.

Oh, my loving Jesus, even in the times when I did not love you, I want to thank and praise you a million times over for your unconditional love for me. My sweet Jesus, I love you. I praise GOD through Psalm 34:1–9 (GNT).

> I will always thank the Lord; I will never stop praising him. I will praise him for what he has done; may all who are oppressed listen and be glad! Proclaim with me the Lord's greatness; let us praise his name together! I prayed to the Lord, and he answered me; he freed me from all my fears. The oppressed look to him and are glad; they will never be disappointed. The helpless call to him, and he answers, he saves them from all their troubles His angel guards those who honor the Lord and rescues them from danger. Find out for yourself how good the Lord is. Happy are those who find safety with him. Honor the Lord, all his people; those who obey him have all they need.

# Chapter 3

## LIFE IN COLLEGE

After completing tenth grade, I entered two years of focused college (pre-degree) at Kuriakose Elias College (KE College), named after Saint Kuriakose Elias Chavara. I chose the science track in order to become a nurse. My sister, Chinnamma Chechy, as I call her, who was practicing as a nurse in the USA, had advised me to do so and encouraged me to study nursing.

While I studied at KE College, my maternal aunt, Kunjamma, as we affectionately used to call her, owned a prestigious restaurant named Rajans. She was a very generous and kind woman. I used to eat breakfast, lunch, and evening snack at this restaurant every day for these two years. Kunjamma used to tell the workers, "Give Lillykutty fresh fried mackerel." I still remember the mouthwatering taste of the food that I had those two years of my college life.

My maternal grandmother, Anna, who lived with my Kunjamma, who is my mom's sister, was very nurturing. After the college class each day, I would always stop by their house, which is also where the restaurant was, and have a snack with tea. One day, I decided not to go to the restaurant and, instead, take the bus straight home. My grandma would always wait for me by the door at 4:00 p.m. when she knew I would pass by, and on this day, she was waiting and called out to me. I told her that I was not coming, but she insisted that I eat first. I refused again and went to the bus stop to wait for the bus.

I stood at the bus stand for one hour, but the bus never came, so I went to my aunt's house. (There was only one particular bus called PTS going through my hometown, and the travel time from my college to my home was about one hour on the bus. In Kerala, all private buses have names.) When I told Grandma what happened, she said the bus did not come because I did not listen to her, but my grandma was happy to see me. Then we ate, and I ended up sleeping at my aunt's house that night.

When I was in eleventh grade, my father had a stroke. I clearly remember that day. On this day, he had decided to take a shower outside, near the well, instead of in the bathroom. It was evening, and I remember it was dark outside because my brothers and I were sitting out on the porch talking. Suddenly, my father screamed my brother's name, "George!" My brothers and I ran to see what was happening. When we got near the well, we saw that my dad was about to fall. My brother got there just in time and caught him. We took him to the hospital. The stroke left him completely paralyzed on his left side. He was in the hospital for one month. With hard work, physical therapy, and care at home with the help of my brothers, my father was able to walk again with assistance. My father's faith remains strong at that time too!

If my father had taken a bath inside the bathroom, we may not have heard him call for help and we may not have been able to catch him before he fell, and he may have sustained additional injuries. Furthermore, we may not have reached him and rushed him to the hospital in time. Looking back, I see that God's providence and protection were ever powerfully present as stated in Psalm 91:11–12 (GNT), "God will put his angels in charge of you to protect you wherever you go. They will hold you up with their hands, to keep you from hurting your feet on the stones." This Word of God truly manifested in my dad's life at that moment.

Upon completing twelfth grade, my sister advised me to apply to nursing school. I wanted to be a teacher in my mind and did not tell anyone but ultimately decided nursing was the best route. I applied to Saint Ann's School of Nursing in Andhra Pradesh, a neighboring Indian state. At the time, my brother Appachan Kunjagala was working in Vijayawada in Andhra Pradesh as a train engineer. Since he lived in the same town as the nursing school, he obtained the application for me. I filled out the paperwork and sent it back to the school.

To get admission, the school needed proof that I had passed my high school studies. When I sent in my application, my test results had not been released. My brother Jose had suggested that I reach out to the Board of Education to have them send my results directly to the college before they were published. That way, I could start nursing school immediately rather than having to wait for a whole year.

A few days later, I received a letter from the director of nursing of Saint Ann's School of Nursing. I opened the letter and was in complete disbelief and shock. I felt lightheaded and thought I would faint. The letter said I had been denied admission to the school because I failed in English in my final exam. Attached to the letter was a copy of my transcript. To pass English, I needed 120 points, but when I looked at the transcript, I only had 80. Where had the forty points gone? I was in disbelief. My brothers and sister all looked at the letter thinking that I was accepted to the nursing school, but when they saw that I had failed English, they did not say a word.

From that day onward, I started to pray on my own in secret. I would get on my knees and cry out to Jesus in one of the bedrooms. I cried out to Jesus, praying, "My Jesus, let me pass when the result comes out publicly." I would pray for this every day.

In our neighborhood, there was a chapel nearby dedicated to Saint Jude Thaddeus, who was one of the twelve apostles and is the patron saint of impossible causes. Saint Jude preached the Gospel of Jesus Christ throughout Mesopotamia, Libya, Turkey, and Persia. He was ultimately martyred. Every Tuesday, I would go to the chapel to participate in the novena prayer to Saint Jude.

In my heart, I felt that getting a passing score on the English exam was an impossible cause. With great tears and plenty of prayers, that summer went by. Every night, I used to dream. That fall, I was attending tutorial college. This is where people would go when they failed a portion of their exams prior to attending college studies. When I woke up, I would be very relieved to realize that it was only a dream! I was still very scared and ashamed to let others know that I had failed because I had passed the tenth-grade finals with first class (honors).

Eventually, the day came when the results were going to be announced publicly. Back in Kerala, our major exam results were published in the newspaper. Each person had an individual number with their corresponding grade listed. At the time, my brother George worked for the newspaper company. That morning, he went to the main office in Kottayam to double-check if I had passed my exams.

My morning was slightly different that day; I woke up, had my breakfast, and went out to the valley in front of our house to get grass for my goats. I had six goats to take care of at that time. I was scared to come home, so I stayed in the valley, caring for my goats. It was almost lunchtime, and I still did not go home. Suddenly, I heard my name. When I listened a bit more closely, I heard that my brother and sister were shouting, "Lilly, come home! Lilly, come home!"

I had a feeling that my brother had come home from Kottayam and told everyone about my results. I was very scared, but I knew I had to go home. I picked up a bundle of grass, put it over my left shoulder so my face could remain hidden, and started to walk home. When I got near the house, I made sure my face was hidden behind the grass. I did this so they could not see my face. I slowly walked toward the porch and looked through the grass to get a glimpse of my family. Through the grass, I saw a bunch of people smiling as I slowly walked toward them. At this moment, I had a good feeling and put the bundle of grass on the ground. My mom, my brothers, and my sister were in a very joyous mood. My dad was lying down in the bed because he was still recovering from the stroke.

I asked everyone, "What is happening?"

My brother quickly responded, "Lilly! You passed!"

I could not believe my ears. When I looked at my official results, I expected to see 80 for English, but it listed 120 as the final score. I was in amazement! That day passed by, and I could not thank Saint Jude enough times. I had faith, but it was not so deep. There was no personal relationship with Jesus. Yet, even then, my Jesus was still taking care of me. This started my special devotion to Saint Jude; when you ask a saint for intercession, they pray to the Lord on your behalf. It is like asking a friend to pray for you; only thing is, these friends are already in heaven. The source of blessing and grace is always from God.

Unfortunately, it was too late to begin nursing school that following semester because admissions had already closed. My family advised me to not waste time and take college courses for one year in the meantime. After a couple of days of thinking and praying, I decided it was better that I used this gap year to take care of my sick father. He was bedridden and needed total care. When I shared this new idea with my family, they were okay with it. Thus, for the first time in my life, I made a life-changing decision on my own, and it was one of the best decisions I ever made.

For one year, I took care of my father's daily needs, including feeding, toileting, hygiene, etc. My brothers would help Chachan shower, and everyone else helped as well. In this way, again by divine providence, I began my path to nursing by helping to take care of my own father.

# Chapter 4

## LIFE AT SAINT ANN'S SCHOOL OF NURSING

After one year, I got admission to the same nursing school, which at first rejected me: Saint Ann's School of Nursing in Vijayawada. The school was run by the sisters of Saint Ann's Congregation, which is headquartered in Switzerland. Most of my classmates were related to a nun at this convent; only three students, including myself, did not have any relatives there. The classmates who had relatives in the convent would visit those sisters during our vacation time from school. There were many convents, and these classmates would go about and visit their relatives. I had been very sad that I had no relatives in the order. When I went home for vacation and expressed this to my brother, he told me that we have a cousin sister in that very congregation named Sister Claret, which I did not know. The good Lord gave me a moment to be proud!

Even though we have so much to study, we all did well in our studies, thanks to wonderful head nurses and professors. Saint Ann's School of Nursing, being a Catholic organization, began each day with Holy Mass and daily prayers before we go to the classrooms, or we go to the hospital for clinical. Many of the faculty members were nuns, and they taught us morals and prayers. In the evening, we would have group prayer at the grotto of our Blessed Mother, and every day we used to pray the Rosary. Everyone in the group cared for one another. We participated in recreational activities like music and dance for special occasions. I also won prizes in sports meets and speech competitions that I took part in while studying at Saint Ann's.

After my second year of nursing school, I got a permanent visa for the United States of America through my oldest sister, Chinnamma Chechy, who had applied for me, and also my siblings. The director of the nursing school, Sister Lima, was so kind and allowed me to have time off for a few weeks to go to the United States to activate my visa. When I came back from the USA to nursing school, they gave me time to study and catch up on the subjects that I missed. They even gave me light clinical duties to complete my studies. I am so thankful and grateful to my professors and the faculty of the nursing school at Saint Ann's, especially to Sister Lima.

Toward the end of my final year of nursing school, my classmates and I saw a movie called *Bala Yesu,* meaning "infant Jesus." This film showed many miracles that occurred in Bangalore, specifically at the Infant Jesus Church. This inspired us to select Bangalore as our destination for our final year excursion. For some reason, our bus driver who drove us from Vijayawada to Bangalore refused to take us to Infant Jesus Church.

All of us were upset, but I remember arguing with the driver, trying to change his mind. Later, during the trip, I saw a man who looked like a priest on a motorcycle who was waving us down. I asked the driver to stop the bus because I thought this priest wanted to tell us something. The bus driver stopped, and this man told the bus driver, "This is not the way to Infant Jesus Church." I was astounded. How did this man know that we wanted to go to Infant Jesus Church? After this miraculous incident, the driver took us to the church. This incident gave me the inspiration to start the devotion to INFANT JESUS. We then visited other parts of Bangalore and the surrounding areas, including the famous Vrindavan Gardens.

At the end of the year, when I graduated from nursing school, my cousin, Sister Claret, drove me to the railroad station and gave me a grand send-off. It made me feel very loved, and I am grateful to my Sister Claret.

My brother, Baby Kunjagala, came to Andhra Pradesh to safely escort me back to Kerala. My sister Kunju Mary Chechy's wedding preparations were underway. During the train ride, Baby Kunjagala was telling me about my sister's future husband; he was a gentleman from a middle-class family. During the preparations for the wedding, my mother told me that she had found a suitable husband for me. I was quite surprised, since I had not thought about my own wedding. I requested my mother to not do any planning until after I had started working in the USA.

After my sister's wedding, she went to America, and after one month, my brother Jose and I followed. It was my second time going to the USA and my brother's first visit. We flew from Kochi to Mumbai, but the airline had a problem, and Jose and I were stuck in the airport for two days. During this time, strangers helped us by giving us emotional and financial support. We received a newfound strength as God's mercy followed us through this incident. Looking back, I thankfully remember this time, my father, and his love for God almighty. I believe it was God's favor on those who honor Him; He gave us the help and the strength we needed at that time. Luke 1:50 (GNT) reminds us, "From one generation to another he shows mercy to those who honor him." The Word of GOD is true and alive.

# Chapter 5

## LIFE IN THE USA

We lived with my older sister Chinnamma Chechy and her family when we arrived in the US. They were kind to us and took care of all our needs. At the beginning of our life in the USA, we did not have much of a prayer life. We would wake up, go to work, come home, watch TV and movies, go to sleep, and then repeat the same thing the next day.

When I came to the United States, I applied to certified nursing assistant (CNA) positions in nursing homes because I had not passed the nursing exam yet. To practice as a nurse in the USA, we as foreign nurses must pass a licensed nursing test called RN (REGISTERED NURSE). Nobody called me back from the nursing homes where I applied for a nursing assistant job. Then I started to pray an hourly novena to the infant Jesus, which I got from Bangalore when we went to see the Infant Jesus Church, as I mentioned in the previous chapter.

This is a special prayer and a powerful novena to the infant Jesus for cases of urgent need. This prayer must be recited at the same time every hour for nine hours consecutively for a special intention. This is that prayer:

Powerful Novena of Childlike Confidence
(This novena is to be said at the same time every hour
for nine consecutive hours—just one day.)

O Jesus,
Who has said, "Ask and you shall receive,

seek and you shall find,
knock and it shall be opened to you,"
through the intercession of Mary,
Thy Most Holy Mother,
I knock, I seek, I ask that my prayer be granted:
(Make your request here)
O Jesus, Who has said,
"All that you ask of the Father in My Name,
He will grant you,"
through the intercession of Mary,
Thy Most Holy Mother,
I humbly and urgently ask Thy Father
in Thy Name
that my prayer be granted:
(Make your request here)
O Jesus, Who has said,
"Heaven and earth shall pass away
but My Word shall not pass,"
through the intercession of Mary,
Thy Most Holy Mother,
I feel confident that
my prayer will be granted:
(Make your request here)
In the Name of the Father,
the Son, and the Holy Spirit. Amen.

I was doing this special prayer for me to get the job, and at the seventh hour, I received a call from a nursing home to come in for an interview. I went in and I got that job. I continued to pray to infant Jesus for anything I needed, but still, I did not have any personal encounter with Jesus yet!

I worked as a CNA for one year. My shift was from 4:00 p.m. to midnight. I used to take the bus home. One day, in 1986, as I was going home from work, I got off the bus around 12:30 a.m. and was walking alone to my sister's house; it was a twenty-minute walk. There was nobody in the street when I got off the bus. Suddenly, I noticed a man following me. I crossed the street, and he crossed it too. At that time, I thought, if he was going to ask me whether or not I was married, I would reply yes even though I was still unmarried. I do not know where I got the courage from at that time.

He came up to me and asked, "Are you married?"

As I had planned, I said, "Yes."

He then left me and said, "Take care!"

That was the first time I heard that phrase. Now I know the HOLY SPIRIT, our helper who is always with us and always guides us, helped me to overcome a dangerous and very tough situation. I was protected by Almighty God. When I told my coworkers about this the next day, my supervisor got very upset and told me, "Do not walk alone anymore," and she proceeded to give me a ride home after every single shift. I am so grateful to my supervisor who treated me like family. This was the beginning of my life in the United States.

God's protective nature was always present in my life. For those of you reading this who do not feel protected or safe, trust that God's presence is with you, and he is indeed protecting you. The wish of God the Father is for all mankind to be saved and to have eternal life. Therefore, God sent his only Son to the world to save us from our sins. The message of salvation was given by Jesus himself. He commanded his disciples to go and teach everyone in the world what he taught his disciples, as written in the Gospel of Saint Mark 16:15–16 (GNT), where he said to them, "Go throughout the whole world and preach the gospel to all people. Whoever believes and is baptized will be saved; whoever does not believe will be condemned."

After Jesus rose from the dead, Jesus appeared to his disciples and taught them again and gave them the courage to proclaim the Good News. In Acts 1:2–5, the Word of God teaches us that the same Jesus who was crucified, buried, and rose after three days appeared to his apostles. It is beyond doubt that he is alive, still teaching and instructing us to teach the people about the kingdom of GOD.

Saul was a well-educated Jew, also a Pharisee, who lived at the same time as the apostles lived. He was killing the followers of Jesus Christ. One day, while he was on the way to Damascus, Jesus called Saul in a unique way to preach the Gospel to many, especially to the

Gentiles. We can read about this incident in the Acts of the Apostles chapter 9. Jesus revealed everything to Saul through the Holy Spirit and gave him instructions to spread the Good News.

Saul, who later became Paul, loved Jesus from his heart and gave up his life for Jesus as a martyr. Saint Paul's second letter to the Corinthians 5:10 (GNT) tells us, "For all of us must appear before Christ, to be judged by him." The message of salvation is freely given to all the people of the world; there is no discrimination. God loves all humans in a unique way, and the salvation is for all, as clearly written in Saint Paul's letter to the Romans 10:13 (GNT), "As the scripture says, everyone who calls out to the LORD for help will be saved."

JESUS is our Lord and Savior, and HE IS THE TRUE GOD. It is the duty of all people in the world to call upon HIM for any need, either physical or spiritual, and also as Christians, it's our duty to proclaim Jesus anytime anywhere. Saint Paul was given this special mission to proclaim Jesus everywhere he went. He did that job well and he always preached about the crucified Christ whom God the Father raised from the dead. Even when he was in prison, he received courage from the Holy Spirit. Jesus was with him all along; Jesus even appeared to him in a dream and talked to him and gave him courage.

GOD the FATHER gave all the authority to his son Jesus, as explained and confirmed through Saint Paul's letter to the Philippians in chapter 2 verses, 10 to 11 (GNT), which tells, "And so in honor of the name of JESUS all beings in heaven, on earth, and in the world below will fall on their knees, and all will openly proclaim that JESUS CHRIST is LORD, to the glory of GOD the FATHER." In our present time, Jesus is continually choosing people to be His witnesses in a remarkable way. In the Gospel of Saint Luke 12:8 (GNT), Jesus says, "I assure you that those who declare publicly that they belong to me, the Son of Man will do the same for them before the angels of GOD." For this reason, I take every opportunity to be a witness to Jesus wherever I am. I will be writing about how Jesus raised me as a witness later in the chapter.

In 1987, as my parents had arranged my wedding, I went back to my hometown in Kerala for my marriage to Johney. The day before my wedding, I took care of my father's grooming, since he was bedridden. When I look back, I know God blessed me because of his mercy, as it's written in Romans 9:16 (GNT), "So then, everything depends, not on what we humans want or do, but only on GOD's mercy." My wedding was a traditional Catholic wedding. On the day of my wedding, I met my husband's sister, who is a missionary nun named Sister Philo Simon, for the first time. When I came to realize that I would now have a sister-in-law who is a nun, it made my day happier. I affectionately call her Kochechy, and my children call her Sister Aunty. I always liked the nuns, and most of my studies were in convent schools. I was attracted to their prayer life.

When I graduated from high school, I had thought about joining the convent, but my father did not agree, and so I had given up on that plan. Now, when I think about that, I realize that God has a plan for each one of us, and it is our duty to discern it in prayer. To understand God's plan for us, we must ask God's wisdom and for the gifts of the Holy Spirit. Wisdom 9:17 (GNT) tells us, "No one has ever learned your will, unless you first gave him wisdom, and sent your Holy Spirit down to him." Without God's wisdom, we are nothing. We must continually ask the Holy Spirit what we are supposed to do each time when we begin something new, and surely the Holy Spirit will reveal to you at that moment what is the right thing. Sometimes, in a difficult situation, when we do not know what to do and we feel helpless, cry out to God and submit to our Savior Jesus and plead for his mercy to pour out upon us.

I went back to America one month after the wedding, while Johney waited two years to come to America due to visa purposes. We exchanged love letters during this time, and our love grew for each other. Once a month, we would call each other. At that time, it was very expensive to call internationally. Soon, my two siblings and I bought a house together, since our spouses had not yet joined us in the US. Even when my husband, Johney, arrived from India, we still lived together in one house. It felt like we were still in India as a joint family. My brother-in-law, Jacob, was the primary chef in the house. He made all the delicious meals for us. We all helped one another with the bills, cooking, and cleaning.

After Johney arrived, I told him how I had miraculously passed the English exam through the intercession of Saint Jude. I wanted a Saint Jude statue, and so Johney took me to a religious store in Flushing. I found the perfect Saint Jude statue and I paid the cashier $20. He packed it in a box very nicely. At that time, Johney told me to open the box and check if the statue was broken or not, but I resisted his opinion and did not open the box at the store. When I got home and opened the box, I was stunned and could not believe my eyes. It was an infant Jesus statue so beautiful that even today, after thirty years, it looks alive! I was shocked but so happy.

At that moment, I realized that I should be putting more emphasis on Jesus rather than the saints.

This is the miraculous infant Jesus statue I got in
the store instead of the Saint Jude statue.

Although the saints are good role models, Jesus Christ is our Lord and Savior. From that day onward, I had a special devotion to infant Jesus. We ask the saints for intercession, but the first place in our heart should go to God the Father and Jesus. At this time, I passed my RN licensure exam and started to work as a registered nurse in the hospital in a medical-surgical unit.

When I was pregnant with my first child, I was working in the hospital. I asked one of the CNAs to do some patient care, but she refused. I reported this to the head nurse. While I was talking to the head nurse, without a warning, the CNA ran up to me and scratched my arm. She got suspended, but she called the union and told many lies about me. A meeting was called for her and me, and my boss asked me if I wanted to get a union representative. I said I did not need anyone because I knew I had not done anything wrong. The CNA continued to lie about me during this meeting. However, I was brave. The director knew I did not do anything wrong, and the CNA was suspended for six months. By the time she returned duty after six months, I was posted on another floor. I would see her in the hallway and I would smile at her and ask her how she was doing. I had forgiven her in my heart.

It is very hard to forgive, but when we forgive the people that hurt us, we are getting special blessings from Jesus. I did not know this before until reading the Gospel of Saint Luke 23:34 (GNT), which stated, "Jesus said, 'Forgive them, Father! They don't know what they are doing.'" This verse manifested in me. So now, whenever people hurt me, I am able to forgive them from my heart. This is a special grace I got from the Holy Spirit. In order to obtain this grace, just meditate on Jesus's passion. Jesus only did good things in this world, and he was killed. He was God himself and came down from heaven as a human being so he could save mankind. We as human beings have not gone through anything compared to what Jesus went through. The way of the cross was the cruelest thing to have ever happened to a human being in this world. And Jesus still forgave the people who killed him. So we must also forgive the people who hurt us physically, mentally, emotionally, and spiritually each and every day. Whoever it may be, just forgive them from your heart. Then you will see the glory of God.

One similar incident also happened when I was working in a nursing home. One night, while on duty at the nursing home, I asked my nursing assistant, who was sitting with another CNA, a floater from another unit, to do some tasks. The floater CNA was angry with me and asked me why I could not do it myself. The task was only to take the audit sheet to the supervisor, a simple task.

Actually, I remember that day like it was yesterday; it was a busy night, and I was giving a blood transfusion to a patient and I did not even take a break. Even though it happened ten years ago, I still remember this incident because usually we do not give blood transfusions that often in the nursing home. I was running around to take care of all my duties without taking a break. I related this incident to my charge nurse and, as per her advice, reported this incident to our night nursing supervisor. The nursing supervisor met with the CNA and did not ask me anything, and then my regular CNA took care of the task.

After two weeks, my supervisor called me to her office and told me that more than twenty CNAs had signed a petition complaining against me to the director of nursing, and she gave that letter for an investigation to the supervisor. I was shocked and speechless. My supervisor asked me to do a self-exam.

"How come twenty people felt the need to complain about you?" she asked. I did not say anything, as I was in shock. When I went home, I was really upset. I took a self-exam and started to write a letter to defend myself. After writing two to three pages in my own defense, I felt in my heart a voice telling me, "If you did everything properly, then you do not need to defend yourself." I was so sad, tears were falling, and I felt an inspiration to open the Bible. I opened the Bible and got to the page of Psalm 3:1 (GNT), which states, "I have so many enemies, LORD, so many who turn against me!"

When I read that whole chapter, tears came from my eyes suddenly, and I felt so much relief and felt calmness and peace in my heart. Right away, I tore up the letter I was writing; I knew it was a retaliation from the CNA, and I felt confident in the fact that I always did my job as a nurse properly. My supervisor never followed up with me regarding this. When you do the right thing, you do not need to be afraid and believe our Lord is always with you and watching over you. I learned from this incident to do the right thing always and depend on God almighty who sees your heart. The Lord will reward you later.

All these twenty-six years of my nursing career, I only once got the achievement award from the psychiatric hospital, but I was not upset. Sometimes, even though you work hard as a nurse, many times I did not get the break when I worked at the night shift as a registered nurse in the hospital and the nursing home too. The authorities may or may not recognize you as the best nurse or give you a "job well done" certificate, but as a nurse, the best award that you receive is from your patients directly. I can tell you honestly from my experience as a nurse. I received a couple of letters from the patient directly saying that my performance made them happy in their difficult time while they were in the hospital. This is the most important award you can receive as a nurse.

The reason I am writing about the award as a nurse is that many get the feeling that no one recognizes us even though we work hard. But I want to tell my friends, if you are a male or female nurse, just do your job the best way, perfectly, and honestly, and then GOD will reward you, He who sees everything. At this time, I want to acknowledge an important message from one of my patients twenty years ago.

I have always tried to provide care to my patients with love and compassion. Twenty years ago, I was working in a medical-surgical unit in a hospital—I still remember what my unit looked like. One day, while I was providing colostomy care for a patient, I asked him to consider colostomy reversal surgery. He replied, "If you were my doctor, I would do the surgery tomorrow!" This left me speechless and honored; it was one of the highlights of my entire nursing career. The role of a nurse is to wholeheartedly take care of the patients entrusted to them, and I'm blessed to have also experienced gratitude from my patient that day.

Our first baby was born on Christmas. My husband and I were ready to go to Christmas midnight Mass. That evening, I started to have contractions. Instead of going to the church, we went to the hospital, the same place where I was working. The doctor in the labor room told me to go back home and that it was not time for the baby to be born. However, I refused to go back home because my heart was telling me to stay in the hospital. I stayed in the lobby of the hospital and was walking around.

During this time, I met my supervisor who was attending the staff Christmas party. She asked me if I wanted any food. I said no but asked her if she could request to the person in charge of the labor room to get me admitted. I remember that it was around 2:00 a.m. She was able to get me admitted, and my baby boy was born around 6:00 a.m. on Christmas day with the umbilical cord around his neck. He did not cry but was grunting. He was immediately admitted to the NICU. Here, clearly I see that infant Jesus saved me and my first-born baby boy from a big dangerous situation! We named him NOEL, which means "Christmas born."

Saint Paul teaches us that all our blessings are from Jesus, not from human effort. At the time, I did not realize this, but now I do. My son came home as a healthy newborn. With God's blessing, we had two more children. Psalm 127:3 (GNT) tells us, "Children are a gift from the Lord; they are a real blessing." At that time, I thank God for my supervisor, Aley, for her intervention in my situation for the glory of God. I learned from this incident that God is watching everything and will take care of all our needs by putting the right person at the right time in our needs. We do not need to worry or get anxious about anything that we go through. We just need to trust in the Lord almighty.

I remember one night, after we all came back from India from our family vacation, everyone was hungry and tired. As my husband and kids slept, I decided to make a pot of rice. I, too, was tired, so as the pot slowly boiled, I decided to lie down on the sofa in the living room and fell asleep. Suddenly, I heard the smoke alarm. When I ran to the kitchen, I noticed that the water had fully evaporated, and the pot was empty and burned. I thanked God for saving us from a very big danger. The Holy Spirit is always teaching us to be united with God.

During those early days, I was working as a registered nurse in the hospital on the night shift. It was difficult for my husband and me to take care of our children since we were working full-time, so my sister-in-law, Aleykutty Chechy, came from India to stay with us and help us raise the children. Those days, we were very blessed and we did not experience much tension or hardship due to my sister-in-law's help. I did not have to cook, just assist in cooking. At this time, I remember Chechy, and I thank God for her life. May her soul rest in peace.

Eventually, my husband and I moved out of the joined family house and into an apartment. Years passed by, and my mother came to live with us. She helped me with the cooking and taking care of the children. My children loved her and her Indian cooking. One night, while she was cooking, she was holding two pots in her hand together. One slipped from her hand and fell to the floor. She took a step and immediately slipped and fell. She tried to get up but was unable to keep her balance. We called 911, and the ambulance came to take her to the hospital. She was admitted, and we soon found out that she had broken her patella.

Just before the surgery, the anesthesiologist suggested that we use spinal anesthesia instead of general anesthesia. I had thought that it would be better if my mother had general anesthesia and I gave the approval for general anesthesia. However, the nurse told me that someone who is in their eighties, as my mother was, should be getting spinal anesthesia only and that I should trust the doctor. I quickly ran to the operation theater and told the doctor to switch back to spinal anesthesia. They did and my mother had a great recovery. After the surgery, my mother was transferred to the nursing home for rehabilitation where I worked. My husband visited my mom in the nursing home every day after his work in the evening. She did two months of subacute rehabilitation, and my husband took very good care of my mother. After about two months, my mother was able to come back to our home and live with us.

When my mother was staying with us, we always did family prayer but not the Rosary. My mother asked me why we are not praying the Holy Rosary. She taught me the importance of reciting the Rosary daily. From that time onward, we would try to pray the Rosary daily.

I want to tell you a brief history of the Rosary. The name *rosary* comes from the Latin word *rosarium*, meaning *"crown of roses"* or *"garland of roses."* Each Hail Mary represents one rose flower, which we give to our Blessed Mother. Mary loves it when we recite the

Rosary, and the devil hates it. Many exorcists have said that the devil has admitted during the exorcism how much Satan hates our Blessed Mother and how the recitation of each Hail Mary is like fire exploding the devil's head. I know for sure that there are many non-Catholics who recite the Holy Rosary for the love of our Lord Jesus and our Blessed Mother. The Rosary is special because the prayers are taken from the Bible itself. The four mysteries of the Rosary allow us to meditate on the life of Jesus, from the annunciation of his birth to his glorious ascension to heaven. It also allows us to reflect on the coronation of our Blessed Mother in heaven. I will be talking more about this in the chapter about our Blessed Mother.

# Chapter 6

## MY JESUS, MY HERO

Acts 10:34–43 (GNT) says,

> Peter began to speak: "I now realize that it is true that God treats everyone on the same basis. Those who fear him and do what is right are acceptable to him, no matter what race they belong to. You know the message he sent to the people of Israel, proclaiming the Good News of peace through Jesus Christ, who is Lord of all. You know of the great event that took place throughout the land of Israel, beginning in Galilee after John preached his message of baptism. You know about Jesus of Nazareth and how God poured out on him the Holy Spirit and power. He went everywhere, doing good and healing all who were under the power of the Devil, for God was with him. We are witnesses of everything that he did in the land of Israel and in Jerusalem. Then they put him to death by nailing him to a cross. But God raised him from death three days later and caused him to appear, not to everyone, but only to the witnesses that God had already chosen, that is, to us who ate and drank with him after he rose from death. And he commanded us to

preach the gospel to the people and to testify that he is the one whom God has appointed judge of the living and the dead. All the prophets spoke about him, saying that all who believe in him will have their sins forgiven through the power of his name."

Revelation 1:6–8 (GNT) says,

**He loves us, and by his sacrificial death he has freed us from our sins and made us a kingdom of priests to serve his God and Father. To Jesus Christ be the glory and power forever and ever! Amen. Look, He is coming on the clouds! Everyone will see him, including those who pierced him. All peoples on earth will mourn over him. So shall it be! "I am the first and the last," says the Lord God Almighty, who is, who was, and who is to come.**

As Christian/Catholics, we know and believe that Jesus Christ died for our sins to save all humanity. Jesus loves everyone in this world equally. He is teaching us to love one another. But there is a question that still remains—whenever I hear news from around the world either through television or newspaper about a crime happening, I sometimes see that the person committing the crime has a Christian name. I am writing this because it hurt Jesus so much. I thought about it a lot, how come people who know Jesus and the teachings of the church do all the bad and evil things, like hurting/killing own family members or innocent bystanders? What went wrong?

And I got an answer from my heart; Jesus gave me that answer in the Gospel of Saint Luke 23:34 (GNT), where Jesus said, "Forgive them, Father! They don't know what they are doing." Yes, it is the truth. If they knew who Jesus was and is, they would not have done the cruel things to Jesus, the same way the people who are in this generation, if they really knew the truth, will not be doing all the terrible/criminal things to their fellow human beings. As a fellow human being/Christian who follow JESUS, what should we do in this situation, and how can we help this poor sinner?

There is only one way if every one of us in this world thinks like this. Due to my weakness, I am not going to hurt anyone; most of us have weaknesses, and we try to hurt other people with our weaknesses. For example, if I say, it's the weakness of a person who has anger, and he gets very angry if he sees something that he doesn't like, in this situation, maybe in the other person's view, it may not be a problem. So to solve this kind of problem, try to talk in a calm way, and the other person will understand better and can avoid a big argument. For whoever has any kind of weakness, first, we have to admit that we may be having some weakness, and we should not take that weakness on other people.

I have experienced and I have witnessed these kinds of behavior in my family and in my workplace too! To prevent this kind of behavior is not easy, and we can't do it by ourselves too! So we should submit all our faults and weaknesses to Jesus's heart through the immaculate heart of Mary. She will give to Jesus's heart, and HE will purify and make us shine like gold. There is another reason that people do not love one another. I found out from the BIBLE IN ISAIAH 29:13 (GNT), where the Lord said, "These people claim to worship me, but their words are meaningless, and their hearts are somewhere else. Their religion is nothing but human rules and traditions, which they have simply memorized."

It is all true, we see that in our own home, in our families, and in our communities too! People do not want to forgive from their hearts; they pretend that they love you, but when the time comes, they will attack you. In order to overcome these struggles, we must learn the most important command Jesus teaches us, "Love God and love one another." Some people will keep everything in the mind and blow up later in a time and look for other people's faults. Instead, think this way—no one is perfect. Try to love God and try to LOVE AND FORGIVE like Jesus did.

When we sin against other people, we are sinning against God. Never forget that Jesus willingly went through the cruel passion to get the salvation for all humanity. The Holy Spirit is teaching us in Saint. Paul's second letter to the Corinthians 5:21 (GNT), "Christ was without sin, but for our sake God Made him share our sin in order that in union with him we might share the righteousness of GOD." Let us meditate on these words: am I hurting anyone with my word, action, or thoughts? How can I be humble? Whenever you make a mistake, say sorry from the heart and forgive from the heart too! And if anyone has different opinions, openly and calmly talk it out instead of blowing out suddenly.

Communication is very important in this matter, for this we need to be open and respect other people's concerns and opinions. Most of the time, if the anger did not resolve in a calm way, it escalates to a different level; even killing sometimes starts with a small argument, and as we have seen in murder cases, it escalated to killing one or another. This is what Jesus is teaching us about anger very seriously. In the Gospel of Saint Matthew 5:23–24 (GNT), Jesus is teaching us, "So if you are about to offer your gift to GOD at the alter and there you remember that your brother has something against you, leave your gift there in front of the alter, go at once and make peace with your brother, and then come back and offer your gift to GOD." And the Holy Spirit is teaching us that constant forgiveness is very important in our daily lives and does not give space to the devil.

God spoke to the people through his chosen prophets. Isaiah was sent by God the Father to speak to his people. God the Father is always watching over his people. Sirach 23:19 (GNT) teaches us that "This man is only afraid of other people. He doesn't realize that the eyes of the Lord are 10,000 times brighter than the sun, that he sees everything we do, even when we try to hide it." During 740 to 700 BC, people were not walking in the truth and were fighting each other (Isaiah 30:8–18). Then God told Isaiah to preach to them (Isaiah 30:19–26). The present generation is no different, as we, too, tend to disobey God's commandments. We as Christians should not follow the movie star, not the sports legend nor the popular singer in the country. Rather, we should follow only one person—Jesus

Christ, the Redeemer of the world, who should be our HERO. When we follow a human being, we are at risk of making mistakes.

Jesus said in the Gospel of Saint John 14:6 (GNT), "I AM THE WAY, THE TRUTH AND LIFE." When we follow Jesus, we do the right thing, both by our actions and by our words. Jesus promised to send us the Holy Spirit. To follow Jesus, we must take up our cross daily, which may be our job, our disobedient children, our inconsiderate spouse, our sick parent, or anyone giving us a hard time—these are our crosses.

To be united with Christ, we must be like Christ who forgave his enemies completely from his heart and loved all mankind without prejudice. We need to be baptized by the Holy Spirit and love Jesus with our whole heart and mind, as Jesus says in the Gospel of Saint John 14:15–17 (GNT), "If you Love me, you will obey my commandments. I will ask the Father, and He will give you another Helper, who will stay with you forever. HE is the Spirit, who reveals the truth about GOD. The world cannot receive HIM, because it cannot see Him or know HIM. But you know HIM, because HE remains with you and is in you."

The Holy Spirit is teaching us through Saint Paul's letter that we are ambassadors for Christ. Second Corinthians 5:20 (NABRE) states, "So we are ambassadors for Christ, as if God were appealing through us. We implore you on behalf of Christ, be reconciled to God." Yes, my dear brothers and sisters, we all are ambassadors for Christ. It is our duty to follow and proclaim Christ in this world. We are in a spiritual battle until the second coming of Jesus. In the diary of Saint Faustina (1488), Jesus said, **"My child, life on earth is a struggle indeed; a great struggle for My kingdom. But fear not, because you are not alone. I am always supporting you, so lean on Me as you struggle, fearing nothing. Take the vessel of trust and draw from the fountain of life—for yourself, but also for other souls, especially such as are distrustful of My goodness."**

We are called to build Christ's kingdom by loving Jesus and our neighbors. How can we do this? The first thing we can do is have a personal relationship with Jesus by speaking and listening to him. Speaking to Jesus looks like talking to a friend, and listening to

Jesus looks like reading the Holy Bible or listening to God's voice in the silence. Another thing we can do is invite the Holy Spirit into our daily lives to lead and guide us. Celebrating the Holy Eucharist regularly will be a rich source of strength for us. Jesus is truly present in the Holy Eucharist and awaits us to come and meet him as he remains in all the tabernacles of the world.

Going to the sacrament of reconciliation (also known as confession) regularly helps us remain in a state of grace, which is very helpful for our lives. In confession, we encounter God the Father's mercy and forgiveness. The priest takes on the person of Christ while forgiving, and it is a very healing and powerful experience. As we need a shower for the cleanliness of our bodies, confession helps with the cleanliness of our souls. The most important part of our body is THE SOUL because the SOUL has to return to God, who created us. In the Gospel of Saint Matthew 10:28 (GNT) says, "Do not be afraid of those who kill the body but cannot kill the soul; rather be afraid of God, who can destroy both body and soul in hell." JESUS is teaching us the most important lesson we should keep in our hearts throughout our life. This lesson is about keeping our soul pure and holy, which leads a person into the state of grace.

Interceding through the Blessed Mother Mary by reciting the Rosary often is also helpful in our lives, as Mother Mary is the mother of God and of everyone. Saint Michael the Archangel is a warrior of heaven; in images, he is normally seen with a sword and crushing the devil. He is known to fight the enemy. He is talked about in the book of Daniel, Jude, and Revelation from the Bible. Pope Leo XIII wrote the prayer to Saint Michael, which is known to be very powerful in defeating evil. During a spiritual sharing session in a charismatic Catholic retreat I attended in 2017, the person I was praying with had a vision of someone carrying a sword standing behind me, so she asked me, "Do you pray the Saint Michael prayer?" And I responded that I did pray it every day. I feel the protection of Saint Michael in my daily life. Here is the Saint Michael prayer:

**Saint Michael the Archangel, defend us in battle. Be our protection against the wicked-**

ness and snares of the devil. May God rebuke him, we humbly pray. And do thou, O prince of the heavenly host, by the divine power of God, cast into hell satan, and all evil spirits who wander throughout the world seeking the ruin of souls. Amen!

All of these SPIRITUAL WEAPONS are available for anyone who wants to grow in their faith in Jesus Christ, defeat evil spirits, and have a closer relationship with Jesus the true God.

Saint Michael the Archangel

Years went by, and we had three children. My husband's niece Sumi and her husband, Jaison, immigrated from India to the US. They stayed with us for a couple of years, and during that time, Jaison, a pharmacist, shared his student life and his spiritual journey with us. He talked about how Jesus changed his life. This really inspired me and encouraged me to grow in my spiritual life.

I was introduced to Shalom TV, a Catholic network (Shalom America and Shalom India, which is broadcasted in the Malayalam language; for English-speaking people, check SHALOM WORLD.ORG). This network carries only faith-related programming, which helps people to grow in their faith and be close to Jesus, which nourishes our soul, the most important part of our well-being. Jesus tells his disciples in the Gospel of Saint Matthew 16:26 (NIV), "What good will it be for someone to gain the whole world, yet forfeit their soul? Or what can anyone give in exchange for their soul?"

## Personal Encounter with Jesus

I attended a Shalom Victory charismatic retreat in 2011. There were many preachers, but one of them was a medical doctor. He talked about having a personal encounter with Jesus. His message deeply touched my heart. This doctor had given up his medical profession for the love of Jesus and become a full-time charismatic preacher to save souls for Jesus. I only remember one thing from that retreat now: "Do not do anything that Jesus does not like." This struck my heart, and I kept pondering it. I had never heard such a teaching before, and it changed my life. And there I personally encountered JESUS. I realized from that moment that I should give God first place in my heart and not do anything that hurts Jesus. Human beings are not perfect, but Jesus's mercy is waiting for each one of us every day.

Throughout the gospel, Jesus teaches his disciples that the most important thing is eternal life and the state of our soul. At the end of time, nothing matters in the eyes of GOD, who we were or what kind of job we held, other than how we lived our life. Did we help the poor? Did we love the poor? Did we do anything for a suffering soul? We can look to the saints who followed Jesus's footsteps and the many martyrs who gave up their lives to keep their faith in Jesus Christ. The martyrs were willing to die in the name of Jesus because of their deeper love for him. And they knew very clearly that Jesus died for them.

Our Catholic Church is enriched with holy martyrdoms and holy saints. They all focused on the crucified Jesus and followed his teaching, they never gave up their faith in Jesus, and, instead, they gave up their lives for Jesus to unite with him in eternity. This is what we are supposed to do as Christians/Catholics—learn the life of Jesus, study the Bible, and only follow JESUS. He is our true hero who gave up the status of God and came down from heaven to bring salvation to all humanity. And it is always our duty to give witness to Jesus wherever we are.

We must follow the truth, and the truth is, Jesus died for our sins and was raised on the third day by God the Father. He appeared to many people, choosing them to be his own disciples. He did the same with me. Jesus is alive in the Eucharist, still living and waiting for me and you in the tabernacle, hiding in the Eucharist. Jesus promised his disciples in the Gospel of Saint Matthew 28:20 (GNT), "And I will be with you always, to the end of the age."

Wherever Jesus is, our Blessed Mother is also there. I remember one seminarian was sharing a fact that his friend seminarian took a picture during EUCHARISTIC ADORATION, AND HE COULD SEE THAT OUR BLESSED MOTHER WAS KNEELING AND ADORING JESUS. I believe that because I know from studying the apparition of our Blessed Mother her main job is to bring back humanity to Jesus, focusing and always pointing us to the Holy Mass and the Eucharistic adoration, where Jesus is present and alive. There's a beautiful quote from Pope Emeritus Benedict XVI on the occasion of the Twentieth World Youth Day in Cologne, which speaks about the EUCHARIST, "Dear young people, the happiness you are seeking, the happiness you have a right to enjoy has a name and a face—it is JESUS OF NAZARETH hidden in the Eucharist. Only he gives the fullness of life to humanity! With Mary, say your own yes to GOD, for he wishes to give himself to you."

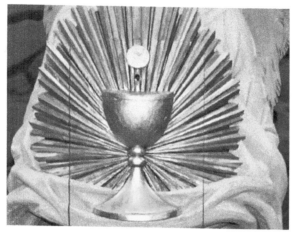

*Host and chalice*

Since I got the personal encounter with Jesus, I try to talk to Jesus as casually as I do to a friend. One random night in 2012, before I went to bed, I asked Jesus, "Can I see your face in my dream?" That night, I saw in my dream a CHALICE AND HOST! Wow, I was looking for Jesus's face as human, but Jesus was teaching me that "I AM THE BREAD THAT CAME DOWN FROM HEAVEN," AS IT IS WRITTEN IN THE GOSPEL OF SAINT John 6:41 (GNT). Additional teachings about Jesus, who is the Eucharistic Lord, can be seen in Saint Paul's writing in 1 Corinthians 11:23–30 (GNT).

> For I received from the Lord the teaching that I passed on to you: that the Lord Jesus, on the night he was betrayed, took a piece of bread, gave thanks to God, broke it, and said, "This is my body, which is for you. Do this in memory of me." In the same way, after the supper he took the cup and said, "This cup is God's new covenant, sealed with my blood. Whenever you drink it, do so in memory of me." This means that every time you eat this bread and drink from this cup you proclaim the Lord's death until he comes. It follows that if one of you eats the Lord's bread or

drinks from his cup in a way that dishonors him, you are guilty of sin against the Lord's body and blood. So then, you should each examine yourself first, and then eat the bread and drink from the cup. For if you do not recognize the meaning of the Lord's body when you eat the bread and drink from the cup, you bring judgment on yourself as you eat and drink. That is why many of you are sick and weak, and several have died.

What a powerful teaching because it was taught by Jesus himself. This is what the Holy Spirit teaches us. Jesus is real and alive in the Eucharist; in diary no. 1288, Jesus is teaching us the importance of receiving the Eucharist in grace through Saint Faustina. Diary no. 1288 states, **"September 19, 1937. Today, the Lord told me, 'My daughter, write that it pains Me very much when religious souls receive the Sacrament of Love merely out of habit, as if they did not distinguish this food. I find neither faith nor love in their hearts. I go to such souls with great reluctance. It would be better if they did not receive Me.'"** So when we receive Jesus in the holy Communion, we must give all the reverence to Jesus because he is GOD himself. That is the reason why the Catholic Church teaches us that we must not receive Jesus if we are in the state of mortal sin, any action that deliberately turns away from God and destroys love in the heart of the sinner. Even if it's only venial sin, a relatively slight sin that does not entail damnation of the soul, it is better we do confession and get repentance from our heart, like what Psalm 51:17 (GNT) teaches us, "My sacrifice is a humble spirit, O GOD; you will not reject a humble and repentant Heart." This is what Jesus is teaching us, to have a repentant heart through confession. And in Saint Faustina's diary no. 1275, Jesus is teaching us the importance of confession. It states, **"My Secretary, write that I am more generous toward sinners than toward the just. It was for their sake that I came down from heaven; it was for their sake that My Blood was spilled. Let them not fear to approach Me; they are most in need of my Mercy."**

Two of the most important things we must do before receiving Jesus in the Holy Eucharist is a self-examination and repenting for our sins. It helps greatly in our spiritual journey; many saints would confess often. I have heard many people say, "I did not do anything wrong, I don't need confession." That is wrong because no one is perfect, but God alone is perfect. This is what the Holy Spirit is teaching us in 1 John 1:5–10 (GNT) regarding the importance of confession to a priest who is the person of Christ:

> Now the message that we have heard from his Son and announce is this: God is light, and there is no darkness at all in him. If, then, we say that we have fellowship with him, yet at the same time live in the darkness, we are lying both in our words and in our actions. But if we live in the light—just as he is in the light—then we have fellowship with one another, and the blood of Jesus, his Son, purifies us from every sin. If we say that we have no sin, we deceive ourselves, and there is no truth in us. But if we confess our sins to God, he will keep his promise and do what is right: he will forgive us our sins and purify us from all our wrongdoing. If we say that we have not sinned, we make a liar out of God, and his word is not in us.

I heard a powerful testimony of a preacher, a Catholic man who was away from his faith for more than twenty-five years. And after attending a charismatic retreat, he went for a confession after twenty-five years. He was a chronic renal failure patient and was at the end stage of life, but he got miraculously healed soon after a full confession, and he became Jesus's witness and disciple. When we have a sincere confession, we get many graces from Jesus through this Holy Sacrament, which the Catholic Church offers. At any time a person requests for a confession, the priest always accommodates the needs of that person. Each time when we are in the confessional, Jesus is present near the priest. This Jesus himself is revealed to many holy people.

God's mercy is new every day and God is light. In the same way, God is asking each one of us to be the light of the world. How can we be God's light to other people? A perfect example is the life of Mother Teresa of Calcutta, who took care of the poor, the oppressed, and the lonely. Mother Teresa told everyone that she got the strength from the daily Holy Mass and was receiving Jesus in the Eucharist daily. The saint's life is a role model for us to lead a holy life because, without holiness, no one can enter the kingdom of heaven. With God's grace and because of their great love for Jesus, the saints did good works on earth, and now they have a special place in heaven.

Blessed Carlo Acutis (1991–2006) loved Jesus so much and loved the Eucharistic Lord. He documented all the Eucharistic miracles that have happened around the world on a website that he created right before he died from leukemia at the tender age of fifteen. From time to time, Jesus gives us Eucharistic miracles for us to deepen our faith in him and to draw us closer to him every day. In the Gospel of Saint John 6:48 (GNT), Jesus teaches us, "I am the bread of life." My dearest friends, Jesus is truly alive in the Eucharist and still living among us. One day, during adoration, I saw Jesus's face in the Eucharist. At the same time, one of my friends from Chicago also saw Jesus's face.

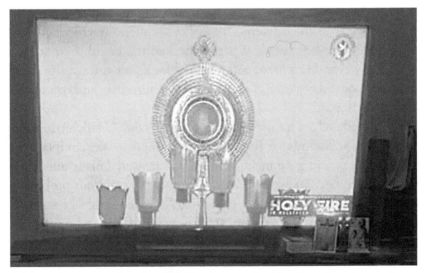

This is the picture I took while I was attending the live adoration online.

Many times, the holy face of Jesus has appeared in the Eucharist; this is one example of a Eucharistic miracle.

In 2012, I was working as a nurse in two different places—one at a nursing home and the other at a psychiatric hospital. Honestly, I did not like to work full-time in either place, so I split my time to do half in each place. I was tired of working nights. I had been working nights for twenty-one years, and the heavy work in the nursing home was getting to me. One night, I woke up around ten forty-five to go to work in the nursing home for an 11:00 p.m.-to-7:00 a.m. shift. As I was getting ready to go to work, I told Jesus, "Jesus, I know millions of people do not have a job in this country and I know that I have a job. Thank you for that, but I don't like my job." After my talk with Jesus, I got ready and left home to the nursing home. Ever since I had a personal encounter with Jesus, I always talk to Jesus like a friend. I knew I had that freedom from Jesus and I could tell him anything.

That same night at work, after midnight, my supervisor called me to come down to the nursing office for an in-service. Because I am a part-time employee, sometimes I would miss the in-service, and the supervisor would give me instructions and teach the current events related to the work I am doing. On the way back to my floor in the elevator, I felt someone is telling me to go to the lowest floor in the building and check for job openings in medical model day care nursing. Next to the cafeteria, there was a bulletin board where job opportunities were posted. When I checked the board, I could not believe my eyes. I saw an opening posted for a part-time position for medical model day care RN on Mondays, Thursdays, Fridays at 8:30 a.m. to 4:30 p.m.

Immediately, I praised the Lord and said, "Hallelujah!" out loud. I was so happy that Jesus heard my simple prayer complaining about my job and gave me an immediate answer! This is our JESUS who loves to hear and respond to our complaints and our problems. He wants to bless us. Psalm 139:1–6 (NABRE) says, "LORD, you have probed me, you know me: you know when I sit and stand; you understand my thoughts from afar. You sift through my travels and my rest; with all my ways you are familiar. Even before a word is on my tongue, LORD, you know it all. Behind and before you encircle me and rest your hand upon me. Such knowledge is too wonderful for me, far too lofty for me to reach." This tells us that God knows us completely. My heart was full of happiness. I submitted the job application form the very next morning, and my supervisor wrote me an excellent recommendation. I ended up getting this job and I knew this was a gift from heaven because after years of doing the night shift and not getting enough sleep, I was getting tired and was feeling weak. Thank you, Holy Spirit, for allowing me to get this job and watching over me so carefully in my day-to-day life!

I was called for the interview shortly after. I have a CGFNS (Commission on Graduates of Foreign Nursing Schools) certification. This means I passed the English and nursing tests given by this organization. Before I went for the interview, I felt inspired to look up the full form of this acronym. I felt that the manager would ask me this question during the interview. The Holy Spirit, my helper, inspired me to check this. He helps us and teaches us everything we need to know in our daily life. To obtain this grace, we must love Jesus and ask Jesus every day to send his Holy Spirit to us. As I had suspected, I was indeed asked this question and I was very happy to answer it correctly! I thank the Holy Spirit and Jesus. Remember to thank God and to acknowledge him for all the favors we always receive!

The Holy Spirit is the third person of the Holy Trinity. He is the helper and advocates that Jesus promised to send from the Father (John 14:15–17). When we feel in our mind or heart a voice or inspiration to do or say something, which is the right thing, that is the Holy Spirit talking to us. He always leads us and teaches us to do good. Jesus tells us again in the Gospel of Saint John 14:25–26 that the Holy Spirit will teach us and make us remember everything that he taught us when he was alive. Sirach 42:15 (GNT) teaches us, "Now I will remind you of the works of the Lord and describe the things I have seen."

I was able to share God's love with my patients and coworkers. Each day with God's grace, I grew in faith and love of Jesus in my daily life by reading the Bible and listening to talks by charismatic preachers on Shalom TV, going to daily Mass, and going for Eucharistic adoration. Years passed by, and I was happy with my job and my life. I never complained about the job and had good coworkers.

In this chapter, I am going to talk about the blessings I received from Jesus, our God and savior, and how those blessings molded me in my spiritual journey. I learned about suffering and how suffering will give us the crown of anointing at the end when we do what is expected of us during our sufferings. When we hear the Word of God, we are hearing JESUS himself. In the Gospel of Saint John 1:1–5 tells us that the Word of GOD is JESUS and that same Jesus is alive and living among us. Again, in the Gospel of Saint John 1:6–18 clearly says who JESUS is and that HE is a true MAN and true GOD.

June 23, 2015, is the day that changed my whole life. On this day, I was diagnosed with breast cancer. At this time, I was drawn into a deeper relationship with JESUS. I learned how one can be very little and I realized that I need God more than anything in the world. After my cancer result came back positive, I was also very positive. I never complained about my cancer and did not feel upset. Through the grace of God, I knew Jesus was going to heal me completely. I praised God for it.

When we praise God and give him thanks in any situation, good or bad, Jesus will take control and work in our life. My husband and my two daughters were home when I told them about my diagnosis. My daughters were strong as I was strong, but my husband cried when I told him the diagnosis. I told him, "This is the first and last time you are crying about this because nothing will happen to me." In my heart, I knew Jesus would heal me completely. The word of God in the Gospel of Saint John 11:40 (NABRE) says, "Jesus said to her, 'Did I not tell you that if you believe you will see the glory of God?'" If you have faith, you will see the glory of God. In Saint Paul's letter to the Romans 8:28 (GNT) tells us, "We know that in all things God works for good with those who love him, those whom he has called according to his purpose."

The Holy Spirit is teaching us a big lesson, and this Word of GOD came alive in my heart. My son was working in another state at that time, and I only told him the diagnosis when he came home.

I did not want my son to get upset, so I told him in a funny way by laughing and said, "I have cancer." Then he said, "Mom, why are you laughing? I have never seen any person who got cancer and laughed about it." Then I told him, "I did not want you to get upset."

The following day, after I received this news, I tuned in to Shalom TV, and a priest was preaching on the topic of suffering. I still remember him saying, "Suffering is not what is given to you but, rather, what God allows in your life because of God's faith in you." Wow! When I heard that statement, I felt GOD was talking to me directly, and I was thinking in my mind how much he loves me, and I received a peace that no human being can give to me. Isaiah 43:11 (GNT) says, "I alone am the Lord, the only one who can save you." It was a powerful word that came into my heart. God allows suffering, he permits it, as it is written in the book of Job. This is what 1 Peter 4:12–19 (NABRE) says,

> Beloved, do not be surprised that a trial by fire is occurring among you, as if something strange were happening to you. But rejoice to the extent that you share in the sufferings of Christ, so that when his glory is revealed you may also rejoice exultantly. If you are insulted for the name of Christ, blessed are you, for the Spirit of glory and of God rests upon you. But let no one among you be made to suffer as a murderer, a thief, an evildoer, or as an intriguer. But whoever is made to suffer as a Christian should not be ashamed but glorify God because of the name. For it is time for the judgment to begin with the household of God; if it begins with us, how will it end for those who fail to obey the gospel of God? "And if the righteous one is barely saved, where will the godless and the sinner appear?" As a result, those who suffer in accord with God's will hand their souls over to a faithful creator as they do good.

These verses teach us why we encounter suffering in our lives. Now I was certain that God had a plan for me and my suffering.

Wisdom 16:12 (GNT) tells us, "No medicine or ointment cured them. They were restored to health by your word, O Lord, the word which heals all humanity." I knew that this happened because God allowed it. When I think about my cancer, if I got this diagnosis before my personal encounter with Jesus Christ, I would not have reacted this way. I would have complained and worried too much. I am afraid that I may even have fallen away from my faith. But Jesus knows me better and what is best for me. As it is written in Psalm 16:1 (GNT), "Protect me, O God I trust in you for safety." Before the surgery, many people prayed for me, and our former parish priest, Father Anto, came into our house, prayed the Rosary with us, and gave me his Rosary to keep. I took the Rosary to the operation theater.

I remember my husband was on his knees the whole time while doing the Rosary. I had confession and also took the anointing of the sick before surgery by the grace of God. All our family and friends were praying for me, and my husband, my children, and my close friend also attended the Holy Mass during my surgery. At the operation theater, there were also my friends who worked there and prayed for me just before surgery. Anything can happen in the operation theater, so we need to depend on the almighty God who is our protector and divine physician and the chief doctor for all doctors in the world. We also need to depend on HIS blessings and mercy on us at all times in whatever we do.

In July 2015, I had the right mastectomy done, and with God's grace, the surgery went well. In August 2015, my husband and I were registered to attend a Catholic charismatic retreat in New Jersey led by Fr. Xavier Khan Vattayil. I could not go for the retreat, as it was only three weeks post-op, but my husband went. I was told by a coordinator of the retreat that I would be able to livestream the retreat for all three days. Jesus gave me the grace to attend the retreat online from the comfort of my home!

The retreat was a great experience, and I felt like I was attending in person at the retreat center. I was joyfully listening to the Word of

God, and it gave me a lot of peace. I also joined in the Holy Mass and the praise and worship sessions. I also followed the exact schedule of the retreat for break times. It is very important to follow the instructions of the retreat preachers. The main preacher, Fr. Xavier Khan, always reminded us to be very attentive, to stay put, and to only leave the retreat hall if it is very urgent because the devil attempts to distract us so that he can steal our anointing. In obedience, I diligently stayed in my seat and was very attentive.

When the Word of GOD is being preached, JESUS will come and visit his people and perform miraculous wonders that will leave people amazed. JESUS himself gave the authority to his disciples to preach the good news to his flock. In the same way, Jesus is asking each one of us to be his witness.

Colossians 2:3 (GNT) states, "He is the key that opens all the hidden treasures of God's wisdom and knowledge." When you have Jesus in you, you do not need anything; everything will be added to your life. We read this in the Gospel of Saint Matthew 6:31–33 (NABRE): "So do not worry and say, 'What are we to eat?' or 'What are we to drink?' or 'What are we to wear?' All these things the pagans seek. Your heavenly Father knows that you need them all. But seek first the kingdom [of God] and his righteousness, and all these things will be given you besides." To obtain this grace, we must have a deeper relationship with Jesus and give HIM first place in our lives and be a witness to him. We must always preach about the kingdom of GOD.

While I was attending the retreat, I heard the message: "Jesus is healing a sister from cancer and raising her as a witness." At that very moment, I knew that was me. I claimed this to be true for myself and thanked the Lord for healing me.

What is meant by *claiming*?

In our faith, we believe that Jesus is giving the messages through the Word of GOD and gives the message for a particular person through the preacher or a spiritual counselor. In charismatic retreats, the Holy Spirit reveals to the preacher a message regarding a particular person and his/her problems and even reveals the name of the person to the preacher. This is because GOD knows each person in the world, whether you are a believer or not. You do not even have to attend the retreat in person to receive the blessings; maybe you are too sick to go for the prayer and your loved ones are going to the retreat and praying for you.

Jesus can heal anytime and in different ways as he pleases because Jesus is God. When you hear a particular message, which you were praying about, that is being announced by the preacher, you can know that the message is from the Holy Spirit. Then you know the message is for you, and you can *claim* it and believe that this is for you or for the one you are praying for. For example, if at a retreat the preacher says, "Someone's arm pain is being healed," and your friend has been experiencing arm pain, you can claim this for your friend and believe that they are healed.

This is what I did when I heard them say, "A sister is being healed of cancer, and Jesus is raising her as a witness." I accepted that message from the Holy Spirit, and at once, I said, "Thank you, Lord, for healing me!" The Gospel of Saint Luke has a beautiful story about a woman who touched Jesus's cloak, and I can relate to it. In the Gospel of Saint Luke 8:48 (GNT), Jesus said to her, "My daughter, your faith has made you well. Go in peace." This teaches us how Jesus heals us through our faith. Faith is the basis of God being able to do miracles. So what is faith? In Saint Paul's letter to the Hebrews 11:1–3 (NABRE), it says, "Faith is the realization of what is hoped for and evidence of things not seen. Because of it the ancients were all attested. By faith we understand that the universe was ordered by the word of God, so that what is visible came into being through the invisible." The most important thing that Jesus teaches us is to have faith in Him and GOD the Father who sent Him. In the Gospel of Saint John 5:19–29 clearly teaches us that Jesus has the full authority over men given by GOD the FATHER.

Six months later, in December 2015, I attended the ANOINTING FIRE Charismatic Catholic retreat, the same retreat team from 2015, which I attended online via livestream, and this time, in person. It was in Florida, and my husband and children accompanied me. I went for this retreat mainly to share my testimony. In the Gospel of Saint Luke 12:8–9 and in the Gospel of Saint Matthew 10:32 teaches us that whoever honors him publicly, Jesus will honor that person before his Father in heaven. I did do the testimony there in Florida; many other people also shared their healing experiences.

Even though I had this spiritual encounter and experience, the doctor ordered a medication called tamoxifen, an oral cancer treatment, for five years. While taking tamoxifen, there is a 1 percent chance for endometrial cancer. Therefore, I was required to undergo abdominal and pelvic sonograms every six months.

After a few months of taking this medication, I started to have irregular bleeding. The doctor performed a sonogram, along with an MRI, to find out why I was bleeding. The MRI showed that I had two polyps in the endometrium. The OB-GYN doctor ordered the polyps to be removed surgically, and the date of the surgery was fixed for July 29, 2016. My daughter Nancy reminded me to take off from work on Friday, July 29, to have the surgery.

I responded, "Anyway, I'm going to attend the retreat. After I come back, I will decide whether I will have the surgery or not." I said this with great conviction because I had a strong feeling that Jesus was going to heal me at this retreat. My daughter got upset and said, "You have to believe the doctors!"

I replied, "I have nothing against doctors." Then I asked my daughter, "Who is my chief OB-GYN doctor?" She did not reply, so I said, "My chief OB-GYN doctor is Jesus." My daughter did not respond but still looked upset. In these difficult situations, we need to have complete trust in the Lord Jesus, and from that moment onward, Jesus will take care of our problems. I am stating this from the experience that I had in this situation.

When you have a deep relationship with Jesus, you can ask him anything, and if it is for the glory of GOD and according to his will, he will grant your request. Now I know everything that happened in my life is GOD's will. Jeremiah 29:11 (GNT) says this clearly: "I alone know the plans I have for you, plans to bring you prosperity and not disaster, plans to bring about the future you hope for."

My husband and I were registered for another retreat by Fr. Xavier Khan Vattayil in Washington from July 14 to 17, 2016. During the retreat, Fr. Xavier Khan was announcing messages from the Holy Spirit. One of the messages was: "Someone sitting here is thinking like this, 'The surgery around the abdominal cavity area has been scheduled, but I'll only decide whether I will have the surgery or not after I attend the retreat.' Jesus is healing this person."

During the retreat, I was sitting toward the front and was very attentive. When I heard that message from the priest, I took it as a sign from the Holy Spirit and was so joyful and speechless; I claimed this grace for myself right away. Immediately, I praised and thanked the Lord almighty for hearing me out. The Holy Spirit taught me that God sees into our hearts and that the Holy Spirit is pleading for his people to God, as seen in Romans 8:27 (NABRE): "And the one who searches hearts knows what is the intention of the Spirit, because it intercedes for the holy ones according to God's will." The Holy Spirit is the leader and master for every retreat.

I was so happy because I knew that person was me. I felt God affirming the conversation I had with my daughter. The Holy Spirit revealed this to the priest and blessed me. Jesus is truly my chief OB-GYN doctor! Not only OB-GYN but also my CHIEF doctor for every department. Since this healing occurred, I always consult Jesus first. God knows our hearts and what we are thinking. God knows you and me personally and sees our hearts. JESUS will not let any person down who trusts in him.

Throughout Jesus's ministry, he was compassionate toward the poor, and Jesus is asking us to do the same. When we care for the poor, Jesus will reward us on earth and in heaven.

Psalm 41:1–3 (GNT) says, "Happy are those who are concerned for the poor; the LORD will help them when they are in trouble. The LORD will protect them and preserve their lives; he will make them happy in the land; he will not abandon them to the power of their enemies. The LORD will help them when they are sick and will restore them to health."

This verse reminds me of my Chachan. I clearly remember his generosity toward the poor, which helped form my own understanding of how I ought to treat the poor. Whenever we serve the poor, we are serving our brothers and sisters and we serve the Lord too. Chachan cared for the poor with much happiness. At the age of seventy-two, he had a stroke and was paralyzed on his left side. He was bedridden for a few months and did not have any complications from the stroke. In fact, he was able to walk with some assistance. Despite the sickness, Chachan was joyful and kept his faith. At the age of eighty-five, my Chachan passed away peacefully at home. He was fully alert and oriented and was able to put his right hand on my son's head to bless him the day before he passed. For me, reflecting on how my father lived and how God was merciful to Him in his sickness is a testament to the goodness of God.

After coming home from the retreat, I called my OB-GYN doctor's secretary and said that I was canceling the surgery. Before she asked me anything, I explained to her that I went for a charismatic retreat and Jesus healed me. I also called the insurance company and made sure they were updated on the canceled surgery. I had already wanted to change my OB-GYN doctor and thought this was a good time to do so. I found a new doctor and explained everything from the beginning, and she was very receptive and suggested that I have a sonogram, which came back negative.

My bleeding got significantly better and then stopped after the retreat. I continued to go for checkups every six months. One time, when I was in the waiting room while I was waiting for a sonogram, I heard people talking about a radiologist who was very compassionate and thorough. For the next appointment, which was scheduled in 2017, I made it with this new doctor.

After this sonogram was done, the new radiologist came out, assessed me, and had a conversation with me. She told me, "Your endometrium is full of liquid. I can't see anything, I have to do a special test called a hysterosonogram." Even though I am a nurse, I never heard of this test. I asked the doctor what this test was and what it was for. The doctor said, "It is to check for polyps."

My mind raced. *Oh, Jesus has already healed my polyps at the retreat. It is good to do this test so that I can have medical confirmation that there are no polyps.*

Within a month, I had the hysterosonogram performed by this radiologist, and she told me, "Your endometrium looks normal, I do not see any polyps, and you only have to come back in one year."

I thanked Jesus in my heart, and then I told the radiologist about what happened prior to this—the breast cancer, the healing experience of the first retreat, the conversation with my daughter, and the healing experience of the second retreat. I shared my witness of what the Lord has done for me to the doctor and I told the doctor, a non-Christian, "Jesus is GOD." It is our duty to proclaim that Jesus is God to everyone we meet in any circumstances. Jesus loves that.

The Holy Spirit gives me the courage to witness that Jesus is the true God in all circumstances. Jesus suffered, died, and rose again, and the apostles witnessed this. When Jesus appeared to the apostles, Saint Thomas, who was not present, doubted that Jesus truly rose again. In the Gospel of Saint John 20:29 (GNT) says, "Jesus said to him, 'Do you believe because you see me? How happy are those who believe without seeing me!'" What a powerful statement from the risen Lord Jesus. When we start to believe in Jesus, there is an inner joy that fills our hearts. We often have idols in our lives. This occurs when we give priority to other things and people over God. A common idol is money. We ought to be very vigilant about the way the evil one wants to trap us in these things. When we entrust our-selves to Jesus, we do not need to be afraid. We see many examples of ordinary people who trusted and followed Jesus. In fact, they became martyrs for the faith and for the love of Jesus. Jesus raised them to his glory. Some of the saints who died for Jesus as martyrs were Saint Sebastian, Saint Peter, Saint Paul, and many more!

How blessed are we that we can receive Jesus in the Holy Communion every day if we choose to? Jesus is alive in the Eucharist. In the Gospel of Saint John 6:48–51, it talks about the Eucharistic Jesus. My readers, if you are confused or do not understand the Eucharist, please read the Gospel of Saint John, chapter 6, and meditate upon it. This is because the Word of God is Jesus. When you meditate upon the Word of God, Jesus Himself will come and reveal His Spirit to you and anything you desire to know. In fact, the Gospel of Saint John 16:13 (GNT) teaches us that "when, however, the Spirit comes, Who reveals the truth about GOD, he will lead you into all the truth." Furthermore, Jesus expressed His sadness to

Saint Faustina in diary no. 1385 regarding how He wants to be more united with His children. Specifically, diary no. 1385 states,

**I desire to unite Myself with human souls; My great delight is to unite Myself with souls. Know, My daughter, that when I come to a human heart in Holy Communion, My hands are full of all kinds of graces which I want to give to the soul. But souls do not even pay any attention to Me; they leave Me to Myself and busy themselves with other things. Oh, how sad I am that souls do not recognize love! They treat Me as a dead object.**

So how can we console Jesus's heart? The answer is quite simple—we just need to invite Him into our hearts and keep Him at the center of our daily life. For example, if you are a student, invite Jesus to come to school with you. If you are working, ask Jesus to help you complete your tasks. If you are cooking, ask Jesus to help you make your dishes and so forth. During these moments and all other moments, the two most important things you can say is, "Jesus, I love you. Jesus, I trust in you." Jesus will love this very much. As it is written in Isaiah 41:10 and 41:13 (GNT), "Do not be afraid—I am with you! I will make you strong and help you; I will protect you and save you. I am the Lord your God; I strengthen you and tell you, 'Do not be afraid; I will help you.'" Jesus is saying that he will always be there for us. It does not matter what circumstances you are facing; he will be there for you. He is inviting us into his sacred heart. There he will give you refuge.

# Chapter 7

## BEING A WITNESS TO JESUS

Don't let me bring shame on those who trust in you,
Sovereign Lord Almighty! Don't let me bring disgrace
to those who worship you, O God of Israel!
—Psalm 69:6 (GNT)

In 2015, Jesus raised me as a witness while attending a retreat. Now I want to tell you how Jesus raised me and how Jesus helped me to be his instrument as a witness.

I will praise you, Lord, with all my Heart;
I will tell of all the wonderful things you have
done. (Psalm 9:1 GNT)

In July 2015, I went to the beauty parlor that I usually go to. I told my beautician that I am diagnosed with breast cancer and will be undergoing cancer surgery on July 30. I usually went once a month to get my eyebrows done, and we would always talk about natural remedies for health. Indian beauticians tend to know a lot about natural remedies, and this is something that always excites me, and I always promote natural remedies for any common cold or small sicknesses.

Even though I went to the beauty parlor many times afterward, she never asked me about my cancer treatment or any personal things. So I also did not say anything about my belief to her because there is always a time for everything, as the book of Ecclesiastes 3:1 (GNT) says, "Everything that happens in this world happens at the time God chooses." Also, Ecclesiastes 3:7 (GNT) says there is "the time for silence and the time for talk." Years passed by, and I went with my daily duties and my nursing job as a registered nurse.

In 2017, Jesus gave me a day to be his witness to my beautician, who is not a Christian and did not know about who JESUS is. One day, in July 2017, I entered the beauty parlor, and as I walked into the common area, the beautician was talking to a customer, saying, "You should drink aloe vera juice," to which the customer said okay before leaving. Afterward, I asked the beautician what is aloe vera juice good for and why she had said that to that customer. She told me, "Lilly, she has cancer and has a poor appetite. By the way, how is your health? How's the cancer?"

Then I told her about my entire journey of healing that I have explained to you all already. She listened very carefully and paid attention and then told me, "I believe in miracles, one of my other customers also told me that she attended a retreat and got healed."

So I asked, "Would you like to come to a retreat with me?"

She replied, "Not me but maybe my daughter." I always invite people to attend a charismatic retreat, since I know the truth about Jesus and the unconditional love that I experienced. In Saint Paul's letter to the Romans 10:17 (GNT), it's clearly teaching us, "So then, faith comes from hearing the message, and the message comes through preaching CHRIST." In all charismatic retreats, the Word of God is shared and preached about Jesus, and the Word of God is JESUS HIMSELF. That we see in the Gospel of Saint JOHN 1:1 (GNT), "In the beginning the Word already existed; the Word was with GOD, and the Word was GOD."

Many conversions are happening when they are hearing about Jesus because Jesus himself opened their hearts to know him truthfully. In the Gospel of Saint LUKE 24:45 (GNT), it says, "Then HE opened their minds to understand the Scriptures." Also, the whole chapter 24 of Saint Luke explained well about the risen LORD and how HE loved HIS disciples even though they all left Jesus alone in his cruel passion (except John). And Jesus appeared multiple times to HIS disciples, giving courage, reinforcing the teaching about HIM, and eating with them, even though they did not believe that JESUS had risen from the dead! Jesus, who had so much patience with HIS own disciples, that same JESUS is calling each one of us to be his witness and disciples too!

Sometimes we get the call, but we did not realize it at that moment. But Jesus is always waiting for us patiently and never gave up on us. Even after two thousand years, Jesus is raised from the dead; he is still calling people to this moment. Jesus himself called me by my name, and I also want others to get that experience of Jesus's love. Jesus himself is inviting people to come to him, all who are tired, labored, and weary, come to him and he will give you rest. In the Gospel of Saint Matthew 11:28–30 (NABRE), it says, "Come to me, all you who labor and are burdened, and I will give you rest. Take my yoke upon you and learn from me, for I am meek and humble of heart; and you will find rest for yourselves. For my yoke is easy, and my burden light."

My beautician told me that her daughter would be calling the next day. My husband and I registered for this charismatic retreat happening this time in New York from August 11 to 13 in 2017. This was being conducted by the same retreat team, the Anointing Fire Catholic Ministry in Kerala, which I had attended previously. Jesus gave me such a joy in my heart that I never felt before, and I left the beauty parlor rejoicing. Jesus gave me a chance to be a witness to him again. Now I know that whenever I speak to someone who does not know JESUS, it is Jesus himself who is opening their heart to listen to me. I give all glory to Jesus our Lord and Savior for opening people's hearts to listen to your works through me, a poor sinner.

My beautician's daughter, Gayathri, later called me, and I shared my testimony with her. She shared with me about what was going on in her life. After hearing her, I knew Jesus would perform a miracle for her family. I briefly taught her how Jesus has immense love and helps those without hope. I asked her if she knew who Jesus was, and she told me, "I don't know Jesus intensely, but I have gone to Catholic churches when I went for vacations just to see how they looked." In the charismatic retreat, the Word of God is preached in the same way as if it was Jesus doing so with his disciples. Jesus said, "When you preach, I will give signs that I am with you." In the same way, when Peter preached the word of God, many miracles happened. Jesus always looked after his disciples. We see this throughout the Bible when we read about the lives of the prophets and the disciples. I later invited her to come with me to attend a Catholic charismatic retreat.

Ever since Jesus healed me from cancer and raised me as a witness, I feel very inspired and joyful to share with others about Jesus's love and mercy, which I encountered. Most of the time, when I meet a stranger or speak with someone one on one—whether that's on an airplane, the doctor's office, or any place—I recall this Bible verse where Jesus told them, "Go out to the whole world and proclaim the Good News to all creation" (Mark 16:15 CCB).

The Holy Spirit gives me the courage to speak about Jesus to others. When I started to write this book, I remembered about Gayathri's healing while attending the retreat in 2017, and when I asked her to be a witness to Jesus and share her story in my book, she was very happy to do it. She was grateful to our Lord Jesus, and with much happiness, she sent me the written testimony about her complete healing and how she received it.

At this time, I remember the Word of God, in the Gospel of Saint Luke 17:11–19, which clearly teaches how important it is to do the testimony and be a witness to Jesus in front of the world to glorify God. When you have no hope and support and you do not know what to do, at that time, Jesus will come into your life and tell you what you are supposed to do. That is what I experienced these past five years from the day Jesus raised me as his witness. In Isaiah 48:17 and Isaiah 40:28–31, it clearly teaches that God is the Lord that controls the universe.

This is Gayathri's testimony:

> Praise the Lord, hallelujah! My name is Gayathri. I know Aunty Lilly through my mom. Aunty used to come to my mom's beauty parlor. And in a casual discussion, Aunty had mentioned

about this retreat happening in New York. Aunty told my mom about the miracles that can happen if you believe in Jesus. I live in Canada, and my mom asked me to come over to New York to attend the retreat. Without giving it a second thought, I took the next flight to New York.

At the retreat, I felt so light and warm and felt like I am at the right place. Hearing everyone talk about their experiences and how miracles happened in their lives was nothing more than a miracle. Thanks to Jesus and Aunty Lilly, I got a chance to speak with Fr. Xavier Khan in person. When I was telling the father about the loss of my baby girl, how I had lost all hope for another baby, and how the doctors had told me that another baby would be difficult, I was in tears. I do not know how, but when Father put his hand on my head for blessing, I started to cry, and right there, I felt that something good is going to happen. And it did. After a year, I got pregnant and gave birth to a beautiful baby boy. All thanks to Jesus, the Almighty, Fr. Xavier Khan, Aunty Lilly, and her prayer groups. Praise the Lord, hallelujah!

This is the testimony of Gayathri, who is not a Christian nor a believer of JESUS. She is still the daughter of GOD almighty. Mainly, what I see in Gayathri is the simple faith of the woman in the Bible from Luke chapter 8, who touched Jesus's cloak and believed that she would get complete healing. In the same way, Gayathri got complete healing from JESUS from her sickness. For that, she is ever grateful to Jesus. Remember, Jesus is the healer, and we are only Jesus's instruments.

The Lord takes lead in our lives and inspires us if we allow Him to. We can do this by inviting Him into our life by simply being vulnerable with Him and speaking to Him from our hearts. It can look as simple as this, "Hi, Jesus. I want you to come into my life and help me, but I have a hard time believing. Please help me." We can also do so by frequenting the sacraments of Holy Mass and confession and spending time in prayer and adoration. These are all helpful to transform one's life into a Christ-centered life. When God comes into our lives, it is natural to want to share His goodness with others because we want them to experience it for themselves, similar to watching a really good movie and telling all your friends to go see it.

God's love is what makes miracles happen, not human efforts. In the Gospel of Saint John 6:44 (CCB), it is written, "No one can come to me unless he is drawn by the Father who sent me; and I will raise him up on the last day." God's will has the final say, so at this time, I want to give glory to God the Father for all of the wonders He has allowed in my life and in those around me. I feel blessed to be able to witness and share God's love and see the miracles He has allowed in my life and others' lives too.

In 2018, after my cancer recovery when I went for a regular checkup at my dentist, Doctor Jack asked me, "Ms. Simon, I did not see you for a long time." Then I told him about how I got cancer and about the journey and healing. Specifically, I told the doctor about how Jesus healed me and raised me as a witness. While I was talking about my cancer journey, I observed that the doctor was paying full attention to my conversation.

I noticed Dr. Jack has been looking very thin since I saw him three years ago. In my nursing observation and assessment, I asked the doctor, "What happened to you, Dr. Jack? It looks like you lost a lot of weight." Then the doctor told me about his medical problems. I promised the doctor my prayers and told him that we will be praying for you in our prayer group too. Then I told him that I would bring back a prayer book that I got at the retreat. The doctor told me, "You can send it with your children the next time when they come for the checkup." When I heard that, I told Dr. Jack that it was no trouble because I lived nearby. I knew this in my heart; I should not delay speaking about Jesus's love and mercy to him because I saw an urgency in his need for healing.

When I came back home, I prayed a Rosary prayer for the doctor and got the inspiration to give out a BIBLE to him. At the retreat, Fr. Xavier Khan instructed us, "If you are going to do anything for Jesus, in order to be fruitful, you must be vigilant, do one Rosary, and pray for that person. The rest, Jesus will take care of it." I saw the fruitfulness of my labor in the intervention, which I had with my dentist, Dr. Jack. When I went back to the dental office the same day, I explained to him about the Bible, how to handle it with reverence and reading every day for half an hour for three months. The doctor was very happy to receive the Bible and the prayer book. Even though the dentist was a non-Christian and does not follow Jesus, he told me, "I am open and believe in miracles that can happen." Jesus is the healer, and we all are his instruments.

I often listen to a charismatic priest's Bible study, and he had said that reading the Bible for a half an hour a day can bring people closer to the Lord. I have heard many testimonies of people doing this for three months and how Jesus has intervened in their lives in a profound way. Jesus is always ready to intervene in our lives, but we ought to invite Him in and give Him the access to do so because He does not force Himself upon us. He knocks at the doors of our hearts. I think reading the Bible and meditating on God's Word help to develop a relationship with God, which, in turn, will change our lives for the better forever. There is a way of praying with scripture called *Lectio Divina*, which means "divine reading." The first step is *lectio*, which means "to read." The next step is *meditatio*, which means "meditation." The next step is *oratio*, which means "prayer." Then next is *contemplatio*, which means "contemplation." And last is *actio*, which means "action." We start by reading the passage from the Bible; you might notice a verse or word that sticks out to you—reread that part and ask the Holy Spirit what it means. Then ask Jesus what He is saying to you personally and specifically through that verse/passage. Respond to Jesus freely, however you'd like to, and try to be as authentic as you can in your response. Remember, Jesus wants you the way you are, not a *perfect* version of you. Then take some time in silence. Some people have said, "Silence is the mother tongue of God." After that, see if there is any action you feel inspired to do in the coming days, which is a fruit of this time of prayer.

I encourage all of you to read the Bible in the morning. It can be hard to find time, but if you can take a short amount of time at the beginning of your day and submit yourselves to God, the King of the universe, and then start your day with trust in the Lord, it can make all the difference! Throughout the day, try to recall the verse(s) you read and how God may be speaking to you through these words; it can lead you in your daily duties and give you the strength you need. Call upon the Holy Spirit in faith by saying, "Holy Spirit, help me," or any other phrase that comes to heart that invites the Holy Spirit. This is for my commuters: whenever you are stuck in traffic or come across road rage, instead of getting angry at the person, bless the person who seems angered; you can use words like, "Lord, please bless them and help them. They don't know what they are doing."

In the evening, you may be tired after a long day at work, but take a cup of tea, sit with God, and tell Him everything. He already knows what you've been through, so if you desire, you can sit silently with the Lord. Open your heart to God. Don't keep anything that's weighing you down within you. We are not meant to go through struggles or any other part of life alone. Share with a friend who can be with you in the situation and also share it with God and give it to Him. This can be done initially by having a conversation with God and then by telling Him that you trust Him with the situation and surrendering all of it (yourself, other people that might be involved, your emotions, the possible outcomes, and the like) to Him. This is confirmed in Psalm 62:5–8 (GNT), "I depend on God alone; I put my hope in him. He alone protects and saves me; he is my defender, and I shall never be defeated. My salvation and honor depend on God; he is my strong protector; he is my shelter. Trust in God at all times, my people. Tell him all your troubles, for he is our refuge."

Jesus is our God and master, and when we depend on him, we do not need to worry about anything that we feel we cannot solve. When we give God first place in our life, Jesus will take over all our needs whether it be physical or spiritual. At this time, we must remember the Word of God. JESUS said, "You could be wrong in this regard because you understand neither the Scriptures nor the power of GOD." (Mark 12:24 CCB)

So what shall we do in any circumstance that is difficult to handle with our human effort? Prayerfully open the BIBLE, and Jesus will talk to you directly and give you a solution, which leads you to peace in your heart in that situation. I have experienced many times this special grace from Jesus by doing this virtue. We must keep all the trust in the Lord who made heaven and earth, like David in Psalm 57:1–3 and 1 Chronicles 16:8–15.

After a few months later, my son went for a regular checkup at the same dentist. Dr. Jack was so happy and shared with my son about his healing and recovery and also how the power of prayer helped him at his most difficult time. He also asked to convey his message to me, and especially how he is grateful for the prayers. Next time, when I went for the regular checkup, he also told me about his healing and acknowledged the power of prayer. He also asked me to keep him in my prayers. Whenever we get a prayer request, I pray for that person especially. I also put the request in the prayer group if it is okay with the person who asked for prayer. We are prayer warriors doing intercession for the whole world. Jesus loves this very much. The doctor was very happy when I asked him about writing a testimony about his healing and the power of prayer. You can read his testimony in his own words.

Below is the testimony by Dr. Jack Gruber:

> In 2018, I was diagnosed with severe diverticulitis and had colon resection surgery. Mrs. Simon, a dental patient of mine and a cancer survivor, told me that she would pray for me. She returned later that day, dropped off a prayer pamphlet, and highlighted a healing prayer for me to recite each day.
>
> I began reciting the prayer on and off on random days as I struggled with my recovery from surgery.

About a month later, another patient came in and asked me if I was all right. It was a strange question, and I asked why. She explained that they had been praying for me at her church. Immediately, I knew this had to be Mrs. Simon's church. At that point, I realized if others could pray for me, I would make it my business to incorporate the healing prayer into my life on a daily basis. After a number of weeks, my healing had rapidly completed.

Praise the Lord! With all my heart I will thank the Lord in the assembly of his people. How wonderful are the things the Lord does! All who are delighted with them want to understand them. All he does is full of honor and majesty; his righteousness is eternal. The Lord does not let us forget his wonderful actions; he is kind and merciful. (Psalm 111:1–4 GNT)

Yes, Lord, I will always proclaim your wonderful deeds, love, and mercy to all of the people I meet. Thank you, Lord, for choosing me to be a witness of your goodness.

Isaiah 12:4–6 (NABRE) says, "And you will say on that day: give thanks to the LORD, acclaim his name; Among the nations make known his deeds, proclaim how exalted is his name. Sing praise to the LORD for he has done glorious things; let this be known throughout all the earth. Shout with exultation, City of Zion, for great in your midst is the Holy One of Israel!"

I want to tell you about a miracle—how Jesus healed my friend's mom. One day, while I was walking on the street, I suddenly thought of my tailor, Seema. I met Seema at the tailor's shop three years prior, in 2018, when I was on vacation visiting my hometown of Kottayam, Kerala, India. On the day that we met, we both happened to be taking the same bus home and got to know each other during the ride. We became friends on that bus. While we had a great time getting to know each other, unfortunately, we had not spoken since that bus ride home.

One day during my daily walks in the Summer of 2021, Seema came into my mind. When I reached home, I immediately called her, and she told me that she was in the hospital with her mom, who needed surgery the very next day. During our conversation, I could sense that she was feeling helpless, as the doctors did not give her any hope regarding the outcome of the surgery. I then talked to her about Jesus, who is the divine Physician, and that he could perform this surgery if she believed. It is through our faith that Jesus can perform miracles. I encouraged her with the Word of GOD from Wisdom 16:12 (GNT), which states, "No medicine or ointment cured them. They were restored to health by your word, O Lord, the word which heals all humanity." Seema and her mother were humble and receptive to the Word of God. I prayed with her over the phone and, with her permission, sent prayer requests to my prayer group, family, friends, and a couple of priests. After the surgery, Seema called me and gave me a full report about her mom's recovery. We can read her testimony below:

> My name is Seema. When I was working as a tailor, I met Lilly Aunty who came by to get her dress fitted. Aunty and I traveled together by bus on our way home. On the journey, we talked about our families, and I told Aunty that I do not have children. Aunty said that she would keep my family in her prayers. Aunty later gave me a prayer book, a Bible, and prayed for me. Then after three years, Aunty called me one day when I was in the hospital with my mother, who was going for a critical spinal surgery the next day. The doctors did not give us any hope and said that the surgery would take eight hours and potentially need additional blood for a transfusion. The doctor even said my mother may die during the operation. With much confidence, my

mom and I agreed for the surgery. Even though my mom agreed for the surgery, her mood was very sad, and she looked hopeless. We did not know what to do and felt desperate. At this time, Aunty called, and suddenly I thought that this was God's intervention. I told Aunty everything. Aunty then talked to my mom and prayed for her over the phone. This gave us hope. Aunty asked us to put our whole trust in Jesus, who is the chief Physician that will perform the surgery. Aunty told us to not be afraid and to trust in Jesus. The surgery was a success and only took four hours. It did not even require a blood transfusion.

The next day, my mom was able to move her leg, which did not have any movement before the surgery. I believe everything was according to God's plan and providence. I take this opportunity to thank Jesus for all the blessings we received in our family through my mother. Jesus, thank you, thank you, thank you!

In 2022, I got a chance to see Seema in her tailor shop in Kerala. She told me that her mom made a full recovery and that she is very grateful that Jesus healed her mom.

# Chapter 8

## HOLY SPIRIT ENCOUNTER

If you love me, you will obey my commandments. I will ask the
Father, and he will give you another Helper, who will stay with
you forever. He is the Spirit, who reveals the truth about God. The
world cannot receive him, because it cannot see him or know him.
But you know him, because he remains with you and is in you.
—John 14:15–17 (GNT)

Even when I had a personal encounter with Jesus, I did not know
much about the Holy Spirit. The Holy Spirit is also a person. When
I was attending a retreat, the preacher was teaching us that Jesus is
a living person and the Holy Spirit is also a living person. The Holy
Spirit is the third person in the Holy Trinity. There is God the Father,
God the Son, and God the Holy Spirit, and when these three persons
are united, it becomes one GOD that is the Holy Trinity. This is a
mystery.

The mystery of the Most Holy Trinity is the
central mystery of Christian faith and life. It is
the mystery of God in himself. It is therefore the
source of all the other mysteries of faith, the light
that enlightens them. It is the most fundamen-
tal and essential teaching in the "hierarchy of the
truths of faith." The whole history of salvation
is identical with the history of the way and the

means by which the one true God, Father, Son and Holy Spirit, reveals himself to men "and reconciles and unites with himself those who turn away from sin. (*Catechism of the Catholic Church*, 234)

We cannot understand the Holy Trinity by ourselves. However, as it is written in the Gospel of Saint John 15:26 (GNT), "The Helper will come—the Spirit, who reveals the truth about God and who comes from the Father. I will send him to you from the Father, and he will speak about me." I want to tell you some of the few encounters that I received through the Holy Spirit.

When I was working as a nurse in the hospital about twenty years ago, I had a patient who was elderly and was terminally ill. One day, my patient asked if we could call her husband after 9:00 p.m. Unfortunately, this was after visiting hours. She had stated, "If you do not call my husband, you will regret it." Suddenly, I had a feeling that she may have felt that she was going to die later that night. I was giving medication at that time and I asked the ward clerk to call the husband. The ward clerk asked me, "Why would we go and disturb the husband?"

I told her, "If you do not call the husband, then I will." The clerk called the husband, and after 10:00 p.m., he came to visit his wife. He was able to spend an hour with his wife before he left. Later, around 4:00 a.m., I came to find out that my patient passed away peacefully. In this incident, even though I did not get a personal encounter with Jesus and I did not hear much about the Holy Spirit, I did not know that we received the Holy Spirit through our baptism and confirmation. Now I know who helped me to make that decision. And I acknowledge the Holy Spirit and I thank him from my heart by glorifying JESUS.

The second story was in 2018, when I went to see my mom in Kerala alone. I wanted to spend some time with my mom; I loved my mom so much. She was ninety-eight years old. When I was in Kerala, I had registered to go for a charismatic retreat about the Holy Spirit anointing in our next town. I heard from other relatives, my cousin sister was sick, so my brother and I went to see her. Actually, I had two important functions to attend that day, one was a birthday party and one was a prayer meeting. With much thought and prayer, I canceled both functions and gave priority to see my cousin, who was sick. When I entered the house, everyone was at home—my aunt, her son, and his wife—and they all were surprised to see me. They asked me when I came from the US, and we casually talked for a while.

Even though everyone's mood was happy, when my cousin sister smiled at me, I could sense that there was some sadness with her. I asked her what happened. She told me that she wanted to go to the Holy Spirit anointing retreat happening next week, but the family would not let her go due to her sickness. As soon as I heard this, I was overjoyed and told her, "Do not worry about a thing. I will take you to the retreat." I got confidence and courage in my heart and told everyone that I had already registered to go for the same retreat, and suddenly, my cousin sister's face lit up, and a beautiful smile could be seen.

When my cousin sister and I talked and prayed in private, she told me that she had been praying to the Holy Spirit to arrange for her to attend this special retreat. She revealed to me her secret of praying to the Holy Spirit. She could not believe that she would be able to go for this retreat. She also told me that she did not know how she would be able to go to the retreat without the consent of her family. I told her to just trust in the Lord Jesus and let us pray together to our dear helper, the Holy Spirit. We did praise and worship privately in her room, and I saw tears coming from her eyes and mine too.

Whenever we cry and pray, Jesus knows how much we love him, and he will never refuse any prayer if it benefits our souls. Sometimes the prayers are not heard because Jesus knows that it is not good for us and wants to give us something better than we asked. I heard it from friends saying that they applied and prayed for a job and did not get it, but when they got the job, it was the best job and company. The only thing we must do is patiently wait and keep praying for God's intervention.

I told my cousin sister that I would take her to the retreat with me and convince the family that I will take care of her during the retreat, and finally, the family agreed, and she was very happy she got to attend the retreat. I was very happy that I was able to take her to the retreat with God's grace. During break time, I bonded with her and observed a fire in her talks, which showed how much she loved Jesus, even in her suffering. During our interaction, she told me about the pain and suffering that she experiences, which she will submit to Jesus for the conversion of sinners. That day, I got more clarity about people who love Jesus and how they love Jesus through their sufferings. Without complaining, they submit their pain and sufferings to the foot of the cross. We must always put our hope in Jesus, who is our LORD and Savior.

I asked how and when she got the personal encounter with Jesus, and then she was very talkative and told me. Since childhood, she got that formation from her grandmother. Her grandma was a pious woman and taught the grandchildren from their early age about Jesus, about how we need to look at heaven and live our lives accordingly. As Saint PAUL said in Philippians 3:20 (CCB), "For us, our citizenship is in heaven, from where we await the coming of our Savior, JESUS CHRIST, the LORD." When she was talking about her grandma's death, she said that everyone that was at the bedside of Grandma saw a light that looked like a ball coming into her face, and she smiled and died very peacefully. Since Grandma's death, she has tried each day to adapt the good qualities of her grandma, to love Jesus and help others.

It was a four-day stay-in retreat, and we were all filled with the Holy Spirit's love and learned more about the Holy Spirit, who is waiting to come and help us when we ask for help. Jesus is also waiting for us to call him. He is knocking at our heart door, and if we open for him, he will come and abide with us and dine with us, too, as he said in the book of Revelation 3:20 (NABRE), "Behold, I stand at the door and knock. If anyone hears my voice and opens the door, [then] I will enter his house and dine with him, and he with me."

In that retreat, we realized how much Jesus loved us and is still loving and living among us. After the retreat, she came home and was overjoyed. Her family even said that she was more energetic and fuller of life, and the next two days, she spent her time calling and talking to her family and friends about this special retreat that she attended.

After two weeks, I went to visit my husband's family in the next town. One night, as I was alone in the room, I went to bed but could not sleep. I remembered that it was after 1:00 a.m., and I was restless in my bed. I never had that kind of feeling, and even I felt my heart was beating fast. So I woke up and did some prayers, praised Jesus, and, after some time, fell asleep. In the morning, when I woke up, I felt that I needed to call my cousin sister's house. When I called the house, her husband picked up and told me that my cousin sister passed away that same night, a little after 2:00 a.m. When I heard the news about her passing, I couldn't believe it. I was able to attend her funeral, and when I looked at her face, I could feel a calmness in her face.

I was thinking that no one knew that this death was coming but Jesus. Jesus knew this was going to happen, and her last wish was fulfilled with God's grace. I am grateful to God almighty for allowing me to travel with my cousin sister on her final days. Jesus always put the right person at the right time; we must always be in union with the HOLY TRINITY. It was the perfect example of my cousin sister's final days, especially by attending a retreat to be with Jesus in prayers, doing adoration, attending Holy Mass, also hearing the Word of GOD preached, and doing a good confession.

Always, during the retreats, the preachers encourage people to have a good confession, and it helps to heal the inner wounds of our hearts. And the most important thing is in Communion with Holy Trinity. In our spiritual journey, it's very important for our soul to be in union with the HOLY TRINITY at the end of our lives because the soul has to return to GOD, who created us. Sirach 2:3 (GNT) tells us, "Stay with the LORD; never abandon him, and you will be prosperous at the end of your days." In this scripture, the Holy Spirit is teaching us that whoever honors God will be blessed at the end of their days.

God knows everything that is happening with us, and nothing will happen without his knowledge. After her funeral, one of her family members told me how happy my cousin sister was after the retreat. They said she spent two days calling her friends and family, telling them how happy she was that she was able to go to the retreat. I even heard after her funeral people talking about how she was very helpful to the family that Jesus entrusted to her and how she took care of their needs and helped anyone who met my cousin sister.

This is what Jesus is asking from us—to "love one another as I have loved you." Jesus always talked about the importance of loving one another unconditionally throughout his ministry. Jesus is love, so as the followers of Christ, we must love one another, especially the people we are in contact with throughout our daily lives.

The Word of God in 1 Peter 1:8–9 (GNT) teaches us how our faith will lead us to eternal salvation, which says, "You love him, although you have not seen him, and you believe in him, although you do not now see him. So you rejoice with a great and glorious joy which words cannot express because you are receiving the salvation of your souls, which is the purpose of your faith in him."

I want to tell a small story about how the Holy Spirit helped me in my physical needs. When I was working as a nurse in the hospital, I registered to go to the diabetic medical conference. I always liked to go to the conferences because we can learn more about the subject. It is also fun because we can go with friends and reconnect with old coworkers from other hospitals that I used to work at.

So at this conference, they were giving out raffles. They were going to do the drawing at lunchtime. When I saw someone getting the gift from the raffle at the table next to mine, I asked the Holy Spirit, if he liked me to get a gift, to let them please call my number next. And as soon as I said that in my mind, my number was called. I could not believe how fast the Holy Spirit heard my simple request. Our heavenly Father will give the Holy Spirit to people who ask about it, as it is written in the Gospel of Saint Luke 11:13 (GNT), "As bad as you are, you know how to give good things to your children. How much more, then, will the Father in Heaven give the Holy Spirit to those who ask him!" The Holy Spirit is our helper in our every need, not only spiritual but also physical needs. The Holy

Spirit is always ready to help us when we call upon him and make sure we acknowledge him in any favors we received.

Whenever I go shopping, I always invite the Holy Spirit to come with me, since I had an encounter with the Holy Spirit and I see a big difference. I recently got a winter jacket with the help of the Holy Spirit. Everyone in my home liked it. Usually, I don't pick up the good things, as I always have trouble picking up good-quality things (I am talking about the dress or jacket). Meanwhile, my husband gets good-quality things for me! But whenever I had help from the Holy Spirit, I was able to choose the best-quality things either for me or for my family. I acknowledge and give all glory to the Holy Spirit at this time, being my helper either physical or spiritual!

# Chapter 9

## PRAYER AND SUFFERINGS

Prayer is an aspiration of the Heart, it is a
simple Glance directed to heaven,
it is a cry of gratitude and love in the midst
of trial as well as joy, finally,
it is something great, supernatural, which
expands my soul and unites me to Jesus.
—Saint Therese of Lisieux

What is prayer?

It is a conversation with God; just like with a good friend, you talk and you listen. God listens, and he speaks with you as well in the depths of your heart. God also speaks to you through the Bible. The Bible is God's words. When you read the BIBLE, it is JESUS himself that is talking to you. In the Gospel of Saint JOHN 1:1 says THE WORD OF GOD IS GOD himself. If you are really looking for a solution to your problem, open the Bible and read it. And Jesus, who is alive and living among us, will speak to you. I have experienced the same.

Once, I was going through some emotional sufferings and I could not sleep, so I woke up around 4:00 a.m. and took the Bible. I closed my eyes and opened the Bible. The passage I got was from Isaiah 50:4–11. As soon as I started to read, tears came from my eyes; I could not control myself and I cried loudly. This incident happened when I was with my mom in 2018 when I visited her. She was in the bathroom that time and heard me cry, and she asked me why I was crying. Until at that time, I did not reveal that incident to anyone, but I told my mom, and she comforted me.

But after reading that Bible passage, I got so much peace and I was able to forgive the people who hurt me emotionally. It is clearly written in HEBREWS 4:12–13 (GNT), which says,

> The word of GOD is alive and active, sharper than any double-edged sword. It cuts all the way through, to where soul and spirit meet, to where joints and marrow come together. It judges the desires and thoughts of the heart. There is nothing that can be hid from God; everything in all creation is exposed and lies open before his eyes. And it is to him that we must all give an account of ourselves.

Jesus said, "Whoever wants to follow me, take up your cross and follow me." I understood what the cross is and how we need to follow Jesus. Actually, Jesus was teaching me about discipleship and how I should take suffering in my life. Prayer and suffering connect like north and south; it goes hand in hand in our life. Hebrews 12:7 (GNT) says, "Endure what you suffer as being a father's punishment; your suffering shows that God is treating you as his children."

The Holy Spirit is teaching us that when suffering comes in your life, you should not get discouraged or lose hope. At the end of that suffering, we will have a resurrection from our Lord Jesus, and we will get the reward from God the Father. We know how Jesus suffered and died for our sins, but after that suffering, God the Father gave all authority in heaven and earth to Jesus by raising him up from the dead. When I see people are getting frustrated, hopeless, or committing suicide, I feel very sad and I want to proclaim to them personally in a loud voice, please have patience. We need to trust in the risen Lord Jesus, who is alive and living among us. We need to talk to him like he is our best friend and listen to him by being silent in his presence. If you can go to a Catholic church, sit near the tabernacle and talk to Jesus about all your problems. We can only trust one person in this world, and that is Jesus. The Holy Spirit will give you inspiration to open the Bible and read, and the WORD OF GOD will speak to you directly and give you a solution to your problems. Many times, I have experienced this powerful solution for my problems. Throughout the holy scriptures, multiple times, Jesus said, "Do not be afraid, for I am with you." Therefore, whenever you feel lonely, hopeless, and afraid, reach out to Jesus. For he says in the Gospel of Saint Matthew 28:20 (CCB), "I am with you always until the end of this world."

In the Gospel of Saint John 14:1 (GNT), it states, "Do not be worried and upset," Jesus told them, "Believe in God and believe also in me." And in verse 6, Jesus is teaching the disciples, "I am the way, the truth, and the Life; no one goes to the Father except by me." In this chapter, Jesus is teaching his disciples that Jesus and God the Father remains in each other. When people look and search for the true living God who is Jesus, Jesus will reveal himself to them, and they will come to know him.

It does not matter who you are and what nationality you are from; do not make your own decisions. When you seek, you will find; when you knock, the door will be opened for you; and when you ask if you don't know who the true GOD is, you will get the answer. Jesus is waiting at your door knocking. So how do we enter these encounters? We do this by hearing Jesus's work and having faith in him. For you to achieve this faith, as Saint Paul said in his letter to the Romans in chapter 10, it teaches us that salvation is for all people, and especially in verse 17 (GNT) which states, "So then, faith comes from hearing the message, and the message comes through preaching Christ."

On the news, I am hearing that more and more people are committing suicide during this COVID-19 time—people around the world and people in the community! Whenever I hear about suicide, my heart weeps for the soul and the family of the individual. I also pray for them. Furthermore, let's look at what Jesus told Saint

Faustina on how we should approach Him when we are desperate. Diary no. **1485 states,**

> My child, do you fear the God of mercy? My holiness does not prevent Me from being merciful. Behold, for you I have established a throne of mercy on earth—the tabernacle— and from this throne I desire to enter into your heart. I am not surrounded by a retinue or guards. You can come to me at any moment, at any time; I want to speak to you and desire to grant you grace. My mercy is greater than your sins and those of the entire world. Who can measure the extent of my goodness? For you, I descended from heaven to earth; for you, I allowed myself to be nailed to the cross; for you, I let my sacred heart be pieced with a lance, thus opening wide the source of mercy for you. Come, then, with trust to draw graces from this fountain. I never reject a contrite heart. Your misery has disappeared in the depths of My mercy. Do not argue with Me about your wretchedness. You will give me pleasure if you hand over to me all your troubles and griefs. I shall heap upon you the treasures of My grace.

**Furthermore, in diary no. 1486, it states,**

> O soul steeped in darkness, do not despair. All is not yet lost. Come and confide in your God, who is love and mercy. My child, listen to the voice of your merciful Father. My omnipotent mercy is active here. Happy is the soul that takes advantage of this grace. What joy fills My heart when you return to me.

Because you are weak, I take you in My arms and carry you to the home of My Father. There is, My child. You have a special claim on My mercy. Let it act in your poor soul, let the rays of grace enter your soul; they bring with them light, warmth, and life. My child, all your sins have not wounded My heart as painfully as your present lack of trust does—that after so many efforts of My love and mercy, you should still doubt my goodness. Here, soul, are all the treasures of My heart. Take everything you need from it. Tell me all, My child, hide nothing from Me because My loving heart, the heart of your best friend, is listening to you."

In Mark 12:24, Jesus taught whatever we need in our daily lives, how to live according to God's law, everything is written in the BIBLE, and Jesus teaches us about how to live in a troubled world throughout the gospel! We need to have a deeper faith in Jesus to overcome all the struggles that we experience in our daily lives, whether it be at home, at work, or in the community. Sometimes we see people who go to church, and they say they are worshiping God and following Christ, but when we get to know them personally, we see a different face. They do not have mercy in them and they do not want to forgive. We see many people like this, but Jesus is teaching us to be merciful like the Father is merciful.

We need to be compassionate to people who are less fortunate than us, be kind to our coworkers, and anyone that we meet on a daily basis. I have seen some coworkers are very rude to others and have favoritism in the same department. Jesus does not like that, and He said, if you have something against your brother, you talk to him alone, not in front of everyone. This we see in Matthew 18:15. Jesus is inviting all people to come to him. Jesus is ready to help them and waiting in the tabernacle, alive; meanwhile, people are looking elsewhere for their satisfaction.

The saints and many people who are living and lived before our time knew the truth about Jesus. And by closing their eyes, they trusted Jesus and depended on God's providence, especially our parents and grandparents. Even though they were not educated, they got the wisdom from heaven and followed Holy Spirit's inspirations. This is the truth about the living God—that we should put God in the center of our lives and give GOD first place in our lives. As it is written in Matthew 6:33, when we seek the kingdom of God and his righteousness, we will be getting all other physical needs.

This is what we need to teach our children from a young age, the power of the God almighty who made this earth and heaven and everything in it. In PSALM 146:1–10, it teaches us that the Lord is the only Savior and he is the king of kings. This is what we need to teach this generation because eternity is forever and Jesus is the same forever. Let's meditate on this Word of God in Hebrews 13:6–8 (GNT), "Let us be bold, then, and say, 'The Lord is my helper, I will not be afraid, what can anyone do to me?' Remember your former leaders, who spoke God's message to you. Think back on how they lived and died and imitate their faith. Jesus Christ is the same yesterday, today, and forever."

There are different forms of prayer—traditional prayers such as reciting the Rosary and all the novenas, praying to saints, different kinds of devotions, and much more. But the prayer Jesus likes the most is the Holy Mass because it is repeating Jesus's passion in the Calvary. Many healings are happening during Holy Mass. Saint Faustina had many visions during Holy Mass, and I got my book title, *My Jesus, My Hero*, during a Holy Mass.

The next prayer that Jesus likes the most is EUCHARISTIC adoration. When we adore Jesus, we are praying and pouring out our hearts to him, even though we are not talking loudly. Jesus, who is alive and looking at our hearts, knows everything about us. Mother Teresa once told a newsman that she got the strength to take care of the sick and abandoned from the daily Holy Mass and one-hour adoration that she spent with Jesus. When I was off one day from work, I got the inspiration to go for the Eucharistic adoration, and that helped me to grow in my faith. I was able to go for adoration every week on Thursday from 12:30 p.m. to 4:00 p.m. at our local parish before the pandemic.

When I see Jesus, I am very happy and I do my prayers. However, most of the time, I fall asleep. And after I wake up, I feel very sad. I was thinking that by sleeping during adoration, I wasted time. This was an ongoing problem, and I always say sorry to Jesus.

One day, something amazing happened during adoration. I started to pray my routine prayers and I fell asleep as I normally do. But as soon as I woke up from sleep, I heard someone reciting the *Hail Mary*. No one was on my bench where I was sitting. I looked around and still saw no one, but I heard it loudly from within my heart; it stayed for a few minutes and stopped. It was an amazing experience. Even when we are weak, the Holy Spirit will help us. He will take over our physical weaknesses and take over our prayers too!

In Romans 8:26–27, it teaches us that in our weakness, the Holy Spirit, our helper, he himself will intercede for us to GOD. Saint Faustina says in the diary no. 73, **"When I feel that the suffering is more than I can bear, I take refuge in the Lord in the Blessed Sacrament, and I speak to him with profound silence."** Jesus loves it when we go and sit in front of him at the Blessed Sacrament when it is exposed.

I want to tell you about how Jesus helps us to connect with other holy people and how their holy life can be an example for anyone to adore Jesus more through their own life. One day, I attended a funeral and I met a young priest who was the pastor of the local Latin church. I knew that they had started Eucharistic adoration, and so I asked the priest if he could increase the days of adoration. He told me that there was not much attendance for the adoration on Monday. He asked if I could come and attend adoration in the church, particularly at 5:00 p.m. on Mondays because at that time, there was only one person in the church. I told the priest that I would come on Mondays from 5:00 p.m. to 6:00 p.m.

One day, when I came out from the church after adoration, there was a lady waiting for me. I had never met her before. She asked for my name and told me her name was Angela. We exchanged phone numbers. She said, "Let us put our names down as adoration

Lilly and adoration Angela in the phone so we can easily recognize the other individual." I thought, *Wow, usually it is I that goes out of my way to meet people to introduce them to Jesus, but Angela found me.* Angela and I grew in friendship and soon became good friends. Months passed by, and we would see each other after our adoration time every Monday at the church parking lot.

Then one day, she told me that she had severe back pain and did not know what was happening. The next time she saw me, she told me that she was diagnosed with cancer. And when I looked at her, I noticed that she was not afraid, nor did she have sadness in her. She was in a lot of pain and she still came for adoration. I saw her dedication to the Eucharistic Jesus, and it gave me more motivation to go for adoration without hesitation. She was a pious woman with integrity and love for Jesus. She offered all her sufferings for the conversion of sinners and the souls in purgatory.

I was very happy to have met Angela. We became good friends and were able to share our spiritual journeys. When she was sick, my friend and I went to her home to recite the Rosary and have fellowship with her. One day, she told me that her son, Daniel, went to traditional Latin Mass and that she would also go with him. She also told me that she went to church every Sunday even though she was in a lot of pain. During our conversations, she especially wanted to talk about her devotion to Divine Mercy Sunday, which she celebrated yearly at her home parish. Divine Mercy Sunday is the special Sunday that comes immediately after Easter Sunday. Many people may not know what Divine Mercy Sunday is. Jesus Himself said these words about Divine Mercy Sunday to Saint Maria Faustina Kowalska.

> **On one occasion, I heard these words: "My daughter, tell the whole world about My inconceivable mercy. I desire that the Feast of Mercy be a refuge and shelter for all souls, and especially for poor sinners. On that day the very depths of My tender mercy are open. I pour out a whole ocean of graces upon those souls who approach the fount of My mercy.**

> The soul that will go to confession and receive
> Holy Communion shall obtain complete for-
> giveness of sins and punishment. On that day,
> all the divine floodgates through which graces
> flow are opened. Let no soul fear to draw near
> to Me, even though its sins be as scarlet. My
> mercy is so great that no mind, be it of man or
> of angel, will be able to fathom it throughout
> all eternity. Everything that exists has come
> forth from the very depths of My most ten-
> der mercy. Every soul in its relation to Me will
> contemplate My love and mercy throughout
> eternity. The Feast of Mercy emerged from My
> very depths of tenderness. It is My desire that
> it be solemnly celebrated on the first Sunday
> after Easter. Mankind will not have peace
> until it turns to the fount of My mercy. (Saint
> Faustina's diary no. 699)

Then again, in diary no. 50, Jesus said, **"I desire that priests proclaim this great mercy of Mine towards souls of sinners. Let the sinner not be afraid to approach Me. The flames of mercy are burning Me—clamoring to be spent; I want to pour them out upon these souls."**

Jesus wants all of humanity to know of his mercy before he comes as KING with all the angels with him in his second coming. What is the second coming of JESUS? The answer is provided in the Gospel of Saint Matthew 25:31–46.

In school, we need to pass final exams in order to move from one grade to the next. To get into heaven, we need to pass judgment to move from the earthly life to eternal life. What is eternal life? Jesus teaches us about eternal life in the Gospel of Saint John 17:3 (GNT), "And eternal life means to know you, the only true God, and to know Jesus Christ, whom you sent." Jesus has given us a guide on how to reach eternal life, which is explained in the Gospel of Saint Matthew 25:31–46. Having a relationship with Jesus, who has shown us how to love the poor throughout his life, will really help us to do the corporal works of mercy, which he asks us to do. Matthew 25:31–46 (GNT) says,

> When the Son of Man comes as King and all the angels with him, he will sit on his royal throne, and the people of all the nations will be gathered before him. Then he will divide them into two groups, just as a shepherd separates the sheep from the goats. He will put the righteous people at his right and the others at his left. Then the King will say to the people on his right, "Come, you that are blessed by my Father! Come and possess the kingdom which has been prepared for you ever since the creation of the world. I was hungry and you fed me, thirsty and you gave me a drink; I was a stranger and you received me in your homes, naked and you clothed me; I was sick and you took care of me, in prison and you visited me." The righteous will then answer him, "When, Lord, did we ever see you hungry and feed you, or thirsty and give you a drink? When did we ever see you a stranger and welcome you in our homes, or naked and clothe you? When did we ever see you sick or in prison, and visit you?" The King will reply, "I tell you, whenever you did this for one of the least important of these followers of mine, you did it for me!"
>
> Then he will say to those on his left, "Away from me, you that are under God's curse! Away to the eternal fire which has been prepared for the Devil and his angels! I was hungry but you would not feed me, thirsty but you would not give me a drink; I was a stranger but you would not welcome me in your homes, naked but you would not clothe me; I was sick and in prison but

you would not take care of me." Then they will answer him, "When, Lord, did we ever see you hungry or thirsty or a stranger or naked or sick or in prison, and we would not help you?" The King will reply, "I tell you, whenever you refused to help one of these least important ones, you refused to help me." These, then, will be sent off to eternal punishment, but the righteous will go to eternal life.

This word of God teaches us the importance of taking care of those that need our help, either physically, emotionally, or spiritually. We must do this with a merciful heart.

Angela and I kept our friendship until she passed away. Then one day, during the COVID-19 season, her daughter texted me that Angela had passed away peacefully in their home. She had received Holy Communion and the last sacraments. Let Angela's soul rest in peace, as well as all other people who died from cancer or COVID-19. Every day, we do pray the Divine Mercy chaplet in our prayer group for all the dying souls. This incident shows how our life is so short in this world. But Angela had the wisdom and knowledge from heaven, and she was looking for eternal life more than earthly life. I could not attend the funeral, but every time I go for adoration, I am reminded of how much she loved Jesus.

Recently, I met Angela's son, Daniel, in the church with his two grandmas. When I saw Daniel brought his grandmothers (his dad's mom and his mom's mom) for the Holy Mass, I was amazed to see a young adult who is taking care of his elderly grandmothers with much enthusiasm. I could see an outpouring of Holy Spirit on Daniel.

After the Holy Mass, I went up to him, and we had a conversation. And he told me since his mom passed, he had started a prayer group once a week with three other young adults in the church. The group now grew up to about twenty people, and most of them were going to be seminarians. When I heard this, I was overjoyed and told him, "Your mom is in heaven and watching over you." He was also happy to see me, and I told him that I was writing this book. When I asked if I could put his mom's story in the book, he gladly agreed. I am sure Angela is watching over me, too, from heaven. I see one truth from this—suffering without complaint will not go to waste, and it will produce fruits in God's time. This is seen in her son, Daniel, who is trying to help young adults to go to the right path and to be a fire for Jesus.

I want to give some thoughts on suffering. Sometimes we think, how come people who are very close to Jesus get suffering? The answer is in Philippians 1:29 (GNT), which says, "For you have been given the privilege of serving Christ, not only by believing in him, but also by suffering for him," and also in 1 Peter 4:12–14, which says that we will get glory after the sufferings from our Lord Jesus. Again, the same is seen in Saint James's letter in chapter 1, verse 12 (NABRE), which says, "Blessed is the man who perseveres in temptation, for when he has been proved he will receive the crown of life that he promised to those who love him."

We will be undergoing different types of sufferings, which can be from physical, mental, and spiritual matters. But when we accept these suffering without complaining, we are doing it for the glory of the kingdom of heaven. These crosses and sufferings that we receive, we are taking for the love of Jesus. Jesus teaches us in the Gospel of Saint Matthew 5:10–12 (NABRE), "Blessed are they who are persecuted for the sake of righteousness, for theirs is the kingdom of heaven. Blessed are you when they insult you and persecute you and utter every kind of evil against you [falsely] because of me. Rejoice and be glad, for your reward will be great in heaven. Thus, they persecuted the prophets who were before you." We just need to follow and accept Jesus's teaching and be faithful to him in our spiritual journey.

Here I want to talk about my mom's prayer life. As I told you in the earlier chapter, my mom's name is Kathreena. She was a very hardworking person, so she did not have time to sit and pray when we were growing up. She used to do the prayer when she did her work. But when she came to the USA, she had plenty of time and she grew in her faith and in her prayer life. It amazed me that when I went to see her in 2018, my mom, who was ninety-eight years old, had an incredible prayer life. As soon as she woke up after the ADL (activities of daily living) and before breakfast, she would pray. She had so many prayer books, which she read daily. Then after breakfast, she would stay in the kitchen to cut any vegetables or anything she could help with and then went back to prayer.

One day, I bought my mom a special prayer book, which contained the fifteen Saint Bridget prayers. The prayer book, *The Prayers on Passion of Jesus Christ,* by Saint Bridget includes this address at the beginning:

> Saint Bridget of Sweden (1303–1373) wanted to know the number of blows our Lord Jesus received during His passion. One day, in the church of Saint Paul at Rome, He appeared to her and said, **"I received 5,480 blows on My body! If you wish to honor them in some way, say fifteen Our Father** ('Our Father, who art in heaven, hallowed be thy name; thy kingdom come; thy will be done on earth as it is in heaven. Give us this day our daily bread; and forgive us our trespasses as we forgive those who trespass against us; and lead us not into temptation, but deliver us from evil. Amen') **and fifteen Hail Mary** ("Hail Mary, full of grace, the Lord is with thee. Blessed art thou among women and blessed is the fruit of thy womb, Jesus. Holy Mary, mother of God, pray for us sinners now and at the hour of our death. Amen') **with the following prayers (which He taught her) for a whole year. When the year is up, you will have honored each one of My wounds!"**

I explained to my mom that this prayer must be recited every day until you complete one year. There were other prayers in the book as well. As soon as I gave the book to my mom, she was so happy and started to read the prayers. Even though she only studied until the fourth grade, she had so much wisdom from heaven. It helped my mom to know the importance of giving God first place in our lives. One day, around 10:30 p.m., my mom was still reading the Saint Bridget prayer book, and I went to see which page she was on. I saw that my mom was reading from the instruction; she used to read the prayers every day like that. She liked to recite these prayers and was very happy and enthusiastic to do so.

My mom loved to read books about saints and any book related to Jesus. The most I loved is that she would invite Jesus to come for all the meals. One day, I heard my mom telling Jesus before lunchtime, "Jesus, today I am going to eat jackfruit. Please come with me." (Jackfruit is a special Kerala dish cooked with coconut, which my mom loved very much.) That conversation amazed me. A ninety-eight-year-old lady was talking to Jesus like a baby. I never did talk to Jesus like that. But from that day onward, I tried to adapt my mom's good qualities in my life, too, but sometimes I was not able to keep it up.

When I visited my mom in 2018, I was blessed to go for two charismatic retreats. Both were Holy Spirit anointing retreats in two different places. At that time, my mom had gangrene on her left big toe. While it was treated with medication, it was not healing. So I told my mom that I would be praying for her healing. During the retreat, there was one-on-one prayer sessions with a gifted counselor. When I was with the counselor, she told me that Jesus is healing the left big toe. At that time, I forgot about my mom's toe and thought I did not have any problems. But that same day, during Holy Mass, the Holy Spirit reminded me that it was my mom's left toe that was getting healed. I immediately claimed it.

When I came to see my mom, my brother told me that the doctors suggested that the only option for the treatment was amputation. However, my mom refused surgery and said, "Jesus will heal me." The left big toe had an open wound, and with medicine and prayer, it got slowly healed. When she was having pain, I asked my mom to offer it for the souls in purgatory. This I learned from holy people.

Also, I told my mom that Jesus was giving her this pain to suffer in this world so that she would not have to go to purgatory. My mom was so happy to hear that statement, which I read from Saint Faustina's diary no. 36. Jesus told Saint Faustina, "**Which do you prefer, suffer now for one day in purgatory or for a short while on earth**." From that day onward, my mom never complained of pain, and she offered all her sufferings to the foot of Jesus's cross for the salvation of souls in purgatory. This is what Jesus is asking from each one of us when we go through any kind of suffering, big or small—to offer all sufferings without complaining to the foot of the cross for the salvation for the souls in purgatory and also for the conversion of sinners in our family and in the world too! Let us see what Jesus is teaching us about how we should handle our sufferings and not waste them. Saint Faustina's diary no. 1032 reads, "**During Holy Mass, I saw the Lord Jesus nailed upon the cross amidst great torments. A soft moan issued from His heart. After some time, He said, 'I thirst. I thirst for the salvation of souls. Help Me, My daughter, to save souls. Join your sufferings to My passion and offer them to the heavenly Father for sinners.'**"

One day, I asked my mom if I could go for the second retreat, which was also in the next town but in a different retreat center, also a Holy Spirit anointing retreat. My mom replied, "Lilly, you just came back from one retreat, why do you need to go for another one?" I told my mom, "If I go, I will bring back the next two volumes of the book, which you are reading, *Through the Eyes of Jesus*." My mom did not know that there were two more books, as she was rereading the first book repeatedly.

The book my mom was reading was *Through the Eyes of Jesus* by C. Allen Ames. It was translated to our native language in Malayalam. My mom was overjoyed about getting the new books, and so she gave me permission. At this time, maybe my readers are wondering why I am going on all these retreats. Let me explain about the Catholic charismatic retreat briefly.

First of all, these charismatic retreats are led by the Holy Spirit, and I have been experiencing Jesus's love through these retreats and blessed with physical healing, as well as spiritual and emotional healing. Also, we are learning the Word of GOD, and it helps us to grow in the virtue of love of GOD and anointing of the HOLY SPIRIT. Mainly, when we are in the retreat center, we are away from home and in a peaceful atmosphere, which helps us to focus on prayer, meditation, and intercession. And there's no need to worry about anything except sit at the foot of the cross and meditate about how much Jesus loved us.

And also, we pray for family members and other people who requested the prayers, especially people who are not able to go for these retreats, which it helped me personally think about eternity more than earthly life. I used to worry a lot before and have some fear about death, but retreats after retreats helped me to overcome these fears, and I was able to focus more on eternity. When we look around us, we see uncertainty for our life and how short our earthly lives are, especially with how many innocent lives have been cut short due to this pandemic around the world. Because of the inspirations I received from the Holy Spirit through these retreats, I was able to start the intercession prayer for the whole world and also invite people to pray with me in the group. The name of our prayer group is *Holy Spirit Our Helper.*

In this prayer group, we have prayed for those who died due to COVID-19 and those affected by COVID-19. We continue to pray for the needs of all the people in the world, for the sanctification of the Catholic Church and all families. We also pray for the dying and those with suicidal thoughts. We pray that sinners would be anointed by the Holy Spirit and also for the other intentions that we are reminded of by the Holy Spirit. If you are inspired to also pray for others, please do so as it is a wonderful gift that you can give to others. Glory be to the Father, to the Son, and to the Holy Spirit.

I will always be grateful to God almighty, which is an act that Jesus loves the most. A PRAYER IS THE BEST GIFT WE CAN GIVE TO ANYONE; ESPECIALLY THOSE PEOPLE WHO DON'T KNOW THAT WE ARE PRAYING FOR THEM. JESUS said many times to pray unceasingly. In

Saint Paul's first letter to the Thessalonians 5:16–18 (GNT), the Holy Spirit is teaching us, "Be joyful always, pray at all times, be thankful in all circumstances. This is what God wants from you, in your life in union with Christ Jesus."

When I reached the retreat center, I was praying to find the second and third volumes of the book *Through the Eyes of Jesus*. The previous retreat center that I went to did not have it, nor was I able to find it in any of the bookstores too! I did not have any problem finding the books in this retreat center with God's grace, and I brought them for my mom. When she saw the books, I saw a beautiful smile on my mom's face; she was so happy. I wanted my mom to be happy, and she loved to read spiritual books. This was the last time I was able to spend time with my mom alive. I asked my mom if she would come with me to the USA, and she told me, "I am not going anywhere from this house, except when I die." My mom showed me her clothes that she wanted to wear at her own funeral, which were packed and put separately in a special suitcase. I know that Jesus gave my mom all the insights about her own death and afterdeath.

My mom told me that she had a vision of Jesus, the Blessed Mother, and angels often. In 2019, on Holy Wednesday, our local parish priest came to my mom's home and gave my mom Holy Communion after hearing her confession. On Holy Thursday, my family always made special bread and milk for the remembrance of Passover. My mom supervised the cooking of the bread and milk, and all the family members and relatives came to have dinner with my mom. Everyone in the family was happy. My mom blessed everyone by putting a cross on their foreheads. We are Syro-Malabar, Eastern Catholics, and this was our tradition, to make bread and milk every Holy Thursday. Then on Good Friday, something unthinkable happened. My mom reminded everyone that on Good Friday, we are to only eat one meal because it was a fasting day for us Catholics.

While going to the bathroom in the afternoon, my mom fell and broke her leg. She was admitted to the hospital in the next town. On Holy Saturday, my mom received the last rites and anointing of the sick and the Holy Communion fully conscious, alert, and well oriented. The priest who came to give the last rites was a young priest, just one year ordained, and he saw my mom's faith and got amazed! After my mom received the last rites, she then put a cross on the priest's forehead and told the priest, "May Jesus bless you, *acchan*." In Malayalam, we call the priest *acchan*. That Saturday, my mom told my brother George, who was at the bedside, "*Velankanni mathave* [our Blessed Mother] with infant Jesus is waiting for me at the door to take me."

My mom passed away very peacefully on Easter. She was ninety-nine years old. My husband and I went to my hometown in Kerala for my mom's funeral. When it was time to get my mom ready for her funeral, no one could find the clothes that she had picked out. My siblings were going to get her new clothes, but I remembered where my mom kept the clothes she wanted to be buried in because she gave me special instructions.

When I found the clothes, I also found the three volumes of the books in that special suitcase, *Through the Eyes of Jesus*. My brother George, who lived with my mom, told me that our *Ammachi* read all three books. In my heart, I was thinking how amazing my mom was. I thank the Lord until now that I was born to such an amazing woman. Every now and then, when I think about her, I miss her, but then I am reminded in my heart that she is now with JESUS!

The third type of prayer Jesus likes for us to do is intercession. This we pray for the conversion of sinners and for whatever need we have. We come together and intercede to our Lord Jesus with special intercession of our Blessed Mother. We have a prayer group called Rosary prayer group, which is connected to our parish. The leader of the Rosary prayer group is our Blessed Mother. I am also a member of this group.

We are all mothers. Some people work night shifts and sacrifice their sleep to spend time in prayer, some people are retired, and some people take the day off just to commit to prayer. We gather to do intercessory prayers for the whole world and for the special needs of the prayer group. We meet every Wednesday at one of the group members' home after the 8:30 a.m. daily Mass at our local Catholic Church. The prayer usually lasts for one hour. Since the beginning of COVID-19, we have been praying on the phone through conference calls. We also participate in online adoration. Since the COVID restrictions are over, we attend daily Holy Mass and Eucharistic adoration in the church.

I am also a member of another prayer group called *Holy Spirit Our Helper*. We pray for all the people in the world. I can honestly say that we are praying for you as well (the current reader of this book), and might I say, may the good Lord bless you in all your needs.

From time to time, the Holy Spirit gives us the inspiration to recite different prayers. Some of these prayers include the Rosary, the Divine Mercy chaplet, Saint Sebastian's prayer, and the Chaplet of Tears. We also read the Psalms and do short praise and worship. If anyone wants to start a prayer group, it is simple. You do not need much—all you need to have is the desire to pray, and Jesus will take care of the rest.

If you do not know how to pray, do not worry. The Holy Spirit will teach you every step of the way. It is written in the Gospel of Saint John 14:26 (GNT), "The Helper, the Holy Spirit, whom the Father will send in my name, will teach you everything and make you remember all that I have told you." The Holy Spirit will inspire you how to start the prayer group and how to end it, and HE himself intercedes for us. All we need is the willingness to pray for the whole world, which also includes those who are oppressed, imprisoned, and those that have no one to pray for them. When we do prayers for others, Jesus will reward us with blessings. In fact, in Saint Paul's first letter to Timothy 2:1–7 (GNT), he talks about the importance of doing intercessory prayers for others. It states,

> First of all, then, I urge that petitions, prayers, requests, and thanksgivings be offered to God for all people; for kings and all others who are in authority, that we may live a quiet and peaceful life with all reverence toward God and with proper conduct. This is good and it pleases God our Savior, who wants everyone to be saved and to come to know the truth. For there is one God, and there is one who brings God and human

beings together, the man Christ Jesus, who gave himself to redeem the whole human race. That was the proof at the right time that God wants everyone to be saved, and that is why I was sent as an apostle and teacher of the Gentiles, to proclaim the message of faith and truth. I am not lying; I am telling the truth!

I want to share the testimony of my close friend Mini. She started the prayer group for mothers in our parish community by the inspiration of the Holy Spirit. She is also a good role model and a prayer warrior herself. She is constantly praying for others in need. The reason I asked her to share her story is to show my readers how prayers are answered for every person; it's a personal and unique experience. Jesus's love is personal and unique in each person.

Below is Mini's testimony:

My name is Mini, a wife and mother of two children with the grace of God who lives a simple life but holds great value for faith and family life. Through my personal encounter with Jesus Christ, I learned to count on the Lord through difficult obstacles in life. Despite the challenges, I have received many graces and blessings that strengthened and renewed me.

Although I received many blessings, I would continue to bargain with God for more and more. At one point in my life, I was struggling with chronic pain in my elbow and had much difficulty performing tasks at work and at home. I would tell Mother Mary, "You were a mother and a woman who knows the difficulties of not being able to do the necessary tasks to raise children who need love and support. So what should I do?" At that time, my daughter was at the age of three, and my son was eight years old.

I had a dream of Mother Mary that resembled a statue placed in my parish church. The statue was Mother Mary holding the child Jesus.

In the dream, I happened to have a tight conversation with her. As I complained, she calmly replied, "Mini, you are always complaining about your pain, don't you see how I struggle to hold Jesus in my hand for you all the time? Please hold this child Jesus for a few minutes." As I received Jesus into my hands, I was undergoing unbearable pain. I told Mother Mary, "You are a statue, and my hand is a real hand with actual pain, are you trying to tease me?"

Suddenly, I woke up and desperately looked around, but I did not see her. However, my chronic pain had disappeared. Despite this wonderful blessing, I continued to complain and say that pain is an abstract thing and there is nothing I could show to people to witness God's true power. People like me need a miracle that really shows a difference or change. I began asking for such a miracle to happen to me.

So it finally happened—my family, my friends, including Lilly Simon, and her husband, also were there at the retreat. And I went for this charismatic retreat by Rev. Xavier Khan Vattayil in Washington, DC, in 2016. It was truly an inspiring, amazing experience in my life. I have been using eyeglasses constantly except when I am asleep for approximately four years. I used eyeglasses for seeing objects from afar. As the years went by, my eyesight began deteriorating, and each doctor's visit resulted in more and more prescriptions. I personally despised wearing glasses, since they were often a nuisance. In spite of this, I begged and prayed to the Lord to free me from this bondage and replenish my vision at least for Holy Mass.

Surprisingly, the *acchan* (priest) announced that he was going to pray for the healing of the eyes and vision. He immediately requested everyone to test their vision with and without eyeglasses then put away their glasses and join the praise and worship. In my mind, I said to myself, *This is not for me because I have been begging the Lord for this healing, and he has not cured me.* I was hesitant to remove my eyeglass at first, but I humbly removed it. I could only see a blurred description of the priest, particularly a big white garment and an oval-shaped circle with no eyes, nose, or lips. He again announced to take the glasses off and pray with him. So I took off my glasses and joined the worship with closed eyes.

During the prayer, I was astonished to see a great light piercing through the roof, which came through a miniature hole, and shining over my head. Suddenly, my head and neck began shaking so fiercely that I had no control over my own body. At this point, it was almost as if I was experiencing an electric shock that had overtaken my entire being. Finally, the praise and worship session was over, and the priest announced, "Please check your visions now." I obeyed and opened my eyes with great disbelief. I was shocked because I could actually see the priest's eyelid movements and lip movements very clearly without my eyeglasses.

Then onward, I have not used eyeglasses for anything except driving. My eye doctor herself said that some good changes have taken place with my vision. This was a new and unique testimony that I could gladly share with the rest of the world, which I have desired for a long time.

When Lilly Chechy (Lilly Simon), one day after the Holy Mass, came up to me and asked, "Mini, would you like to share your story of the healing of your eyes into my book?" I got very happy and surprised. I never thought she would ask me this; I knew she was writing the book because actually I was praying for this particular incident to be revealed to the world, but I did not know how it could be. I had sent this testimony to the retreat center. But in Jesus's time, I take this opportunity as the confirmation from the Holy Spirit, and my intention is only to glorify the Holy Trinity. I can share through my experience that we have an amazing God. This unique experience was eye-opening for my life, and it gives me a strong desire to keep God at the center of my life.

Prior to this experience, God always has been part of my life, but my success and pride have distanced me from him. My prayer life has improved drastically. I can effortlessly begin my day with thirty minutes of Bible reading, going for daily Mass, and having confession monthly. I also pray from the heart the daily Rosary and the Divine Mercy chaplet at least twice a day. It has been and continues to be a routine in my daily life. Through God's grace, two prayer groups were initiated—one in my city after the healing of the pain in my arm (Lilly Simon, the author of this book is part of the group) and another at my workplace after the healing of my eye.

The only purpose and intent of all this is to show and prove that God is alive and active and that the experience of God's presence is much precious compared to physical healing itself. He is always ready to come down to us and prove his love for us. As Psalm 145:9 (RSVCE) states, "The LORD is good to all, and his compassion is over all that he has made." Let us be thankful for all he has done in our lives and continue to praise and worship him through our actions.

We have to see how faith and action are related to each other. Without action, the faith is dead. And without faith, the action is also dead. It is written in the letter of Saint James chapter 2:22 (NABRE), "Was not Abraham our father justified by works when he offered his son Isaac upon the altar? You see that faith was active along with his works, and faith was completed by the works."

# Chapter 10

## THE BLESSED MOTHER

I am not only the Queen of Heaven, but also the mother of Mercy.
—Our Lady to Saint Faustina

**"If We separate ourselves from the Mother of God, we are separating ourselves from Our God Who Created us."** On December 1, 2020, I heard this quote when I was sleeping, and I woke up to Jesus's voice.

Most of us in the world have heard about Mary, our Blessed Mother, but some of the readers may not know about this special woman from heaven. God the Father chose this special lady to be his Son's mother, and now she is also our mother. Jesus himself gave Mary to us to hold on to until he comes back in the second coming. We are blessed to have a mother in heaven to intercede for us to God the Father and her Son Jesus and also her beloved spouse, the Holy Spirit. God sends his daughter Mary to earth to convince people who do not believe in God the Father, the Son Jesus, and her beloved spouse, the Holy Spirit, and that salvation is only through her Son Jesus. As it is written in Romans 10:8–13 (NABRE): "But what does it say? 'The word is near you, in your mouth and in your heart'" (that is, the word of faith that we preach), for if you confess with your mouth that Jesus is Lord and believe in your heart that God raised him from the dead, you will be saved. For one believes with the heart and so is justified, and one confesses with the mouth and so is saved. For the Scripture says, "No one who believes in him will be put to shame." For there is no distinction between Jew and Greek; the same Lord is Lord of all, enriching all who call upon him. For "everyone who calls on the name of the Lord will be saved."

I just want to give some thoughts on our Blessed Mother and how she is helping people to prepare around the world for Jesus's second coming. There is much proof that shows our Blessed Mother's apparition on this earth. There is evidence; it is not a myth, it is the truth, which I also experienced in my pilgrimage to the holy places where our Blessed Mother appeared to the people, mainly children, who are very poor and innocent.

Mary is the mother of God, who is Jesus. She is also the mother of all people. She is mentioned multiple times in the gospels and has appeared in many places in the world. I would like to tell you more about this amazing woman who changed my life and all of humanity's lives forever. Since I am not a writer, I always ask Jesus and the Holy Spirit for inspiration on what to write in this book. I want to share something very beautiful. The other day, on November 30, I was writing about a quote that I found in the church bulletin from my local parish. It was from Saint Basil and it was about the Blessed Mother, and I already had put it in at the end of this chapter.

When I was writing that, I thought that so many saints are saying very nice things about our Blessed Mother. I do not have a quote for myself, actually, as I was talking to Jesus in my mind. I completed this chapter and went to bed. In the early morning of December 1, 2020, at four thirty, I heard a gentle voice, which I believe was the Lord Jesus's, in my sleep about the Blessed Mother. I could not sleep anymore, and I was reciting this quote repeatedly in my half-sleep. I thought that I should write this down right away in case I forget it. The quote was like this, **"If we separate ourselves from the mother of God, we are separating ourselves from our God who created us."** I was so joyful and wrote it down on a piece of paper as soon as I woke up. I was amazed at how Jesus is hearing even my small thoughts. Psalm 139:1–6 clearly teaches us that God knows everything about us.

So let us love Mary as our own mother. When Jesus was on the cross, he gave us the right to call Mary our mother. Our Blessed

Mother has so many titles. The most important title is "Queen of Heaven and Earth." Jesus is the King of kings, and the Mother of the King has a very important role in the kingdom of heaven and earth. Whatever the Queen asks of the King, the King will never refuse. We are very blessed to be able to call Mary our own heavenly Mother. She will never refuse anything we ask for if it is according to God's will.

For the rest of this chapter, I want to explain a few qualities of our Blessed Mother.

## Annunciation

In the Gospel according to Saint Luke, we learn about Mary. Luke 1:26–38 (NABRE) says:

> In the sixth month, the angel Gabriel was sent from God to a town of Galilee called Nazareth, to a virgin betrothed to a man named Joseph, of the house of David, and the virgin's name was Mary. And coming to her, he said, "Hail, favored one! The Lord is with you." But she was greatly troubled at what was said and pondered what sort of greeting this might be. Then the angel said to her, "Do not be afraid, Mary, for you have found favor with God. Behold, you will conceive in your womb and bear a son, and you shall name him Jesus. He will be great and will be called Son of the Most High, and the Lord God will give him the throne of David his father, and he will rule over the house of Jacob forever, and of his kingdom there will be no end." But Mary said to the angel, "How can this be, since I have no relations with a man?" And the angel said to her in reply, "The holy Spirit will come upon you, and the power of the most high will overshadow you. Therefore, the child to be born will be called

holy, the Son of God. And behold, Elizabeth, your relative, has also conceived a son in her old age, and this is the sixth month for her who was called barren; for nothing will be impossible for God." Mary said, "Behold, I am the handmaid of the Lord. May it be done to me according to your word." Then the angel departed from her.

Humanity received salvation through Mary's yes. Mary was fully human, immaculately conceived in her mother's womb. This means she did not have the stain of original sin. Mary was very devout and close with God. So when the angel Gabriel appeared to her, she responded with an honest inquiry, "How can this be?" followed by openness and acceptance to God's will, "Behold, I am the handmaid of the Lord. May it be done to me according to your word."

Reflection: Have you nurtured your relationship with God? Have you spent time in daily prayer, where you talk and listen to the Lord? Mainly in our silence with God, we can hear God speaking to us. We need lots of patience, so let's all pray for that virtue!

From a young age, the Blessed Mother formed me as her daughter from my parish church activities. We were members of the sodality and missionaries of little flower in my hometown in Kerala. We recited the Rosary prayer daily. We helped our parish by praying for others and encouraged other children to be part of the parish community. I really enjoyed it because everyone in the community knew one another and helped one another. However, when I came to the USA, things changed, and I grew a little distant from our Blessed Mother and forgot about her partially. I did not have a devotion and did not say the Rosary for years. But when my own mother came to live with us in the USA, she saw that we were not doing the Rosary and asked, "Lilly, how come you are not reciting the daily Rosary, which is an essential part of our family prayer back home?"

This is what a mother does—when her children are not doing the right thing, she brings them back to the right path. In the same way, our Heavenly Mother is always watching us. She wants us to do the right thing. She even has the authority from God the Father to appear in different parts of the world to the people. And the message conveys that we repent, sacrifice, and do penance for poor sinners, mainly conversion of heart. She wants all people to know her Son JESUS is the true God and Savior for all people.

To find Jesus, we must repent from wrongdoing and purify our hearts with prayer, sacrifice, and penance. Then we will be able to remove the chains of oppression and the yoke of injustice and let the oppressed go free. We should also share our food and homes to the poor and homeless, clothe the naked, and love everyone, especially our family members and relatives. There we will find Jesus in all people that we meet.

When we are obedient to God's will, the Holy Spirit will give us the wisdom to choose the right thing. When the Holy Spirit comes, you will know right from wrong, and you will recognize the right things to do and will be able to know the will of God in our life.

## Visitation

Our Blessed Mother is a walking tabernacle and the Ark of the Covenant carrying Jesus everywhere she goes. She helps others in need by carrying Jesus and adoring constantly. When Mary was carrying Jesus in her womb, she visited her cousin, Elizabeth, who was also carrying John the Baptist in her womb. When Mary greeted Elizabeth, the baby in Elizabeth's womb leaped for joy, as he knew he was meeting his Lord and Savior. Wherever there is the presence of Jesus, the Holy Spirit will also be there. No one revealed to Elizabeth that Mary was carrying Jesus, but the Holy Spirit, who knows everything in our heart, revealed the truth to Elizabeth.

## Nativity

In this situation, we see our Blessed Mother as a young teenager, who totally and blindly believed in God's providence, saying, "Here I am, your handmaid. What a humility we see here, for that she sang the Magnificat" (Luke 1:46–55).

## Presentation

Here we see our Blessed Mother in the temple where she was presenting Jesus to GOD the Father, along with Joseph, her husband. The prophet Simeon was praying to see the Messiah whom GOD the Father promised to send for the salvation of all mankind. As soon as he picked up the baby, the Holy Spirit revealed to him that this baby is GOD's Son, the Messiah, whom Simeon had been waiting for all of his life to see. Simeon the Prophet gave glory to God Almighty and told Mother Mary a sword will pierce her heart. Luke 2:25–35 clearly teaches WHO JESUS IS.

## Wedding at Cana

In this event, we see our Blessed Mother, who was interceding and pleading to JESUS, her son, for a family who was about to get shamed in public. Even though it was not time for Jesus to perform his miracle, Jesus respected his mother and showed the world that his mother's word was very valuable to him. This is the same way when our Blessed Mother intercedes for each one who seeks her help. She intercedes to Jesus, her son. I heard from an exorcist that the devil is revealing the truth about our Blessed Mother, how heaven loves Mary, how she got all authority to help people in need, and how God the Father loves her very much.

We see that both the mother and the son respect each other and listen to God the Father. When the mother instructs the servants (at the wedding of Cana) to listen to Jesus, she takes a step back and shows the world that her Son is greater than she is. This shows that the Blessed Mother is always leading us to her Son Jesus.

## Carrying of the Cross, at the Foot of the Cross, and Crucifixion

In the suffering of Jesus, our Blessed Mother never left her Son. She walked with him. She showed him her presence in silence. She prayed that he would get the strength to carry the cross, which bore the weight of our sin. Where there is a cross, God will also send down his graces to you. From the foot of the cross, Jesus told his disciple, John, who was the only disciple that stayed with Jesus until Jesus's death, to take care of his mother. In John 19:26–27, it shows Jesus giving his mother to John. This actually means that Jesus gave the world his mother. She is the mediator between Jesus and all mankind. Our Blessed Mother suffered with Jesus on the way to Calvary.

*Jesus on the Cross*

## Assumption/Coronation

In this beautiful ceremony in heaven, the coronation of the Blessed Mother happened. It happened with God the Father, God the Son, and God the Holy Spirit, along with millions of angels and saints. Our Blessed Mother reached heaven as soon as she died, and the angels carried her whole body to heaven.

Mary is the mother of God, but she is also our mother. In the Gospel of Saint John 19:25–30 (NABRE), it says,

> Standing by the cross of Jesus were his mother and his mother's sister, Mary the wife of Clopas, and Mary of Magdala. When Jesus saw his mother and the disciple there whom he loved, he said to his mother, "Woman, behold, your son." Then he said to the disciple, "Behold, your mother." And from that hour the disciple took her into his home.

This was one of the last words of Jesus and, therefore, extremely vital. It may seem like Jesus is simply entrusting Mother Mary to his disciple, but this was also the moment Jesus gave his mother to all humankind.

A mother is probably the best supporter, along with the father for a child. Jesus knew it would help us to have a perfect mother that we can cry out to. When Jesus walked to Calvary, his mother, Mary, walked with him. This provided great consolation to JESUS. Jesus and Mary knew that this was the plan of the heavenly Father. So Mary supported her son Jesus to complete his mission in this world. She helped to fulfill the Father's desire, to save mankind from sin and bring them back to salvation, which mankind lost at paradise due to Adam and Eve's disobedience to God by submitting to temptation.

When God created this world, he saw everything was good, though God saw something was missing. So he created human beings in his own image and likeness.

> Then God said: Let us make human beings in our image, after our likeness. Let them have dominion over the fish of the sea, the birds of the air, the tame animals, all the wild animals, and all the creatures that crawl on the earth. God created

mankind in his image; in the image of God he created them; male and female he created them. (Genesis 1:26–27 NABRE)

Sin came into the world through pride and disobedience to God and the devil's jealousy. Some examples of sin are hurting people mentally, physically, and spiritually. Other examples include killing babies in the womb, killing people, stealing, marrying the same sex, and much more that we see in Galatians 5:19–21 (GNT), where the Holy Spirit teaches us,

> What human nature does is quite plain. It shows itself in immoral, filthy, and indecent actions; in worship of idols and witchcraft. People become enemies and they fight; they become jealous, angry, and ambitious. They separate into parties and groups; they are envious, get drunk, have orgies, and do other things like these. I warn you now as I have before: those who do these things will not possess the Kingdom of God.

The Holy Spirit is teaching about the devil's trap. Therefore, 1 Peter 5:8 CCB says, "Be sober and alert because your enemy the devil prowls about like a roaring lion seeking someone to devour." Evil is all around the world, and in order to defeat the devil, we need to be dependent on our Blessed Mother's help. God the Father gave the authority to the virgin Mary to be the mother of the SON OF GOD to crush the devil's head as we read in GENESIS 3:15 (GNT), "HER offspring will crush your head." We also need to stay close to Saint Joseph, who is the foster father of Jesus. Additionally, the devil is terrified to hear Saint Joseph's name, so we need to keep Saint Joseph as close to us as we can. In order to stay away from all sins, we need the grace from God the Father, and for that, we must always be in union with the Holy Trinity.

The Gospel of Saint Matthew 18:6–9 (GNT) says,

> If anyone should cause one of these little ones to lose his faith in me, it would be better for that person to have a large millstone tied around his neck and be drowned in the deep sea. How terrible for the world that there are things that make people lose their faith! Such things will always happen—but how terrible for the one who causes them! If your hand or your foot makes you lose your faith, cut it off and throw it away! It is better for you to enter life without a hand or a foot than to keep both hands and both feet and be thrown into the eternal fire. And if your eye makes you lose your faith, take it out and throw it away! It is better for you to enter life with only one eye than to keep both eyes and be thrown into the fire of hell.

Jesus teaches his disciples about the seriousness of sin, who causes sin, the consequences of sin, and how to avoid sin. Those who cause others to sin are just as sinful. Some people are weak, and some people take advantage of people that are weak. Some people may have no one to listen to their problems, even in their own family. This is what Jesus is saying—we must be merciful to our families and neighbors and love them. We must forgive them constantly. Without God's grace, we cannot do anything.

How can we help a person in such a situation? Only through communication and guidance from the Holy Spirit. This is what happens in a spiritual sharing. For example, if someone does not want to tell you everything for whatever reason, that is completely fine because Jesus knows everyone's heart. In spiritual sharing, which usually happens at a charismatic retreat, Jesus will reveal to the counselor all the problems of the induvial in front of them. Most of the time, the people with inner wounds are healed by doing a full confession. In Saint Faustina's diary (1448), Jesus said,

> **Write, speck of my mercy. Tell souls where they are to look for solace; that is, in the Tribunal of Mercy [the sacrament of reconciliation] There the greatest miracles take place [and] are incessantly repeated. To avail oneself of this miracle, it is not necessary to go on a great pilgrimage or to carry out some external ceremony; it suffices to come with faith to the feet of My representative and to reveal to him one's misery, and the miracle of Divine Mercy will be fully demonstrated.**

And also, in diary entry no. 723, Jesus said, **"I perform works of mercy in every soul. The greater the sinner, the greater the right he has to My mercy."** Jesus says the same thing in the Gospel of Saint Luke 5:32 (NABRE): "I have not come to call the righteous to repentance but sinners."

I experienced a beautiful encounter with Jesus while I was in spiritual sharing with a preacher! In order to clarify this matter about the spiritual sharing, I want to tell you about myself. When I was pregnant with my fourth child, the baby died in the womb at one month, and I got a miscarriage! I did not tell anyone except my immediate family. When I went for a retreat, the preacher, who was a lay missionary, revealed to me, "Jesus wanted to give you one more baby, but you did not get it." When I heard this message from this preacher, I was amazed at how Jesus wants me to get inner healing from this sadness! I always wanted a fourth child! The preacher told me to offer Holy Mass for the baby who died in my womb, which I never did before. This opened my eyes and heart even more to Jesus. Jesus knew everything about me and revealed to me how to get peace.

After this, we offered a Holy Mass for the baby and named the baby Nova, and I felt so much peace in my heart. The Holy Spirit is the retreat master and guides the preachers. It is important that we go for a retreat at least once a year. We must also go to confession as often as we can. We can see what Jesus told Saint Faustina about confession in her diary (entry 1602), where she writes,

> Today the Lord said to me, "Daughter, when you go to confession, to this fountain of My mercy, the blood and water which came forth from My heart always flows down upon your soul and ennobles it. Every time you go to confession, immerse yourself entirely in My mercy with great trust so that I may pour the bounty of My grace upon your soul. When you approach the confessional, know this, that I Myself am waiting there for you. I am only hidden by the priest, but I Myself act in your soul. Here the misery of the soul meets the God of mercy. Tell souls that from this fount of mercy, souls draw graces solely with the vessel of trust. If their trust is great, there is no limit to My generosity. The torrents of grace inundate humble souls. The proud remain always in poverty and misery because My grace turns away from them to humble souls.

As I mentioned before, all people are God's children. Mary is the daughter of God the Father, and she is also the mother of Jesus, the Son of GOD.

Mary is the daughter of Joachim and Anna. Her parents conceived in their later years, and God blessed them with a child that was Mary. One of her titles is the Immaculate Conception. This means that God the Father kept Mary from original sin to prepare her to be the mother of the SON OF GOD. The Son of God is the second person in the HOLY TRINITY, and the Holy Spirit is the third person in the HOLY TRINITY. The Holy Spirit is also the spouse of the blessed virgin Mary.

Gabriel is one of the archangels, a special messenger from God to humans.

I'd like to say that the virgin Mary's response to the angel Gabriel is one of the most important words ever found in the Gospel of Saint Luke 1:38 (NABRE), "Behold, I am the handmaid of the Lord. May it be done to me according to your word." These words were her yes to God, and it changed humanity forever. All of humanity has been affected by her yes.

## Testimony

The Blessed Mother has appeared in many places to different people! The Church calls these Marian apparitions. Some of these places include Fatima in Portugal, Lourdes in France, Medjugorje in Bosnia, Rosa Mystica in Italy, and so on. I was able to visit a few of these places such as Guadalupe, Medjugorje, Fatima, Lourdes, Rosa Mystica, and Velankanni. I just want to write about my experiences in a few of those places that I visited with my family.

*Guadalupe*

In 2017, my brother-in-law, my sister-in-law, my husband, and I went to Guadalupe, along with our friends, on a pilgrimage. This is a place in Mexico where Mother Mary appeared to the native people of nonbelievers. At that time, the people in Guadalupe were doing human sacrifices and adoring idols such as the sun and the moon as their GODS. The people who lived there were poor and illustrated. Heaven saw that God's children were dying and that they did not know who the true God was. Whenever there is more sin, there will be more grace poured out to God's people from heaven. This is the perfect example that we will see in our Blessed Mother's apparition in Guadalupe.

While we were walking through the moon pyramid and exploring the place, our spiritual guide asked us to recite the Divine Mercy chaplets for the millions of victims who were killed in this place so long ago. We eventually reached a flat surface where there were no trees and plants. The moon pyramids were built for performing ritual sacrifices of humans and animals. All this time, we were praying the Divine Mercy. At the conclusion of the prayer, I was able to smell a sweet fragrance that was coming from the top of that area. I never experienced a smell like this in my life. It was better than perfume! I asked my friends if they could smell the same thing, and they came closer to where I was standing and were able to smell the same fragrance. Our tour guide was also standing nearby and told us that this was the presence and is evidence that our Blessed Mother is standing next to us.

I was so happy, and so were my friends. This past summer in 2020, I went for a walk and I wore a mask due to the COVID-19 situation. I was reciting the Rosary while I was walking, and then I smelled rose flowers. I stopped for a moment and looked around if there was any rose plant nearby, and I could find no rose plant in any yard. Then I was so happy, for I understood at that moment that our Blessed Mother was walking with me. This was the second time I experienced the presence of the Blessed Mother. Our Blessed Mother is very happy when we recite the Rosary prayer because it's Jesus's life itself!

From December 9–12, 1531, a big miracle happened in Guadalupe, which changed all of Mexico City. Our Blessed Mother was sent by God the Father to save his people from their sins. Our Blessed Mother appeared to Juan Diego, who is a person with a deep faith in God. He was on his way to morning Mass when our Blessed Mother appeared to him on Tepeyac Hill, and the rest of the story is history. The apparition is described as that of a young woman with black hair and darkened skin. Mary said to Juan Diego, "I am your merciful Mother, the Mother of all. Do not be troubled or weighed down by grief. Do not fear any illness, anxiety, or pain. Am I not here who is your Mother? Are you not under my shadow and protection? Am I not your fountain of life? Are you not in the folds of my mantle? In the crossing of my arms? Is there anything else you need?"

Each time, when there is a Marian apparition, there will be a goal and mission from heaven. By 1541, just ten years after our Blessed Mother apparition appeared to Juan Diego, a historian of that time wrote that nine million people in Mexico had converted to Catholicism in a nonbloody way, and they discovered the truth of the incarnation! This is what we are seeing in all Marian apparitions. Our Blessed Mother is the messenger of heaven even in our present time.

Our Lady of Guadalupe

*Medjugorje*

On October 2, 2019, my husband, my cousin from Switzerland, other pilgrims, and I went on a pilgrimage to Medjugorje. There, Mother Mary appears every month on the second and twenty-fifth day. We were all waiting in the valley of a small mountain to see the apparition of our Blessed Mother.

This is the picture of our Blessed Mother of Medjugorje.

There were more than twenty-five thousand people waiting for Mother Mary's apparition. These people were all reciting the Rosary when suddenly we heard a woman in the crowd crying. Her cries soon turned into screams for help. She said, "Help me, help me," in Italian. She began to shout, "Why are you coming here? There is no one here to see you. Go to purgatory! There will be no marriages here, and there will be a lot of divorces!"

I looked around to see what was happening and saw two priests from another group raising their Benedictine cross and praying toward the sound coming from the lady. We could not see the woman because there were so many people, but we heard her sound very loudly! After a short time, the woman's voice became calm, and we could not hear her anymore. During this time, our Blessed Mother appeared in the sky, and many people saw her in the clouds, and a few people in our group were able to smell a sweet fragrance when our Blessed Mother arrived. The time was between 8:00 a.m. and 9:00 a.m. We all left the place with so much happiness in our hearts and praised God almighty for his love toward mankind. Our Blessed Mother has a different role and purpose for each place she visits! Mainly at Medjugorje, there are many conversions happening to this day!

Later that evening, I went to church for confession. There I met two young women from England who asked me if I knew what the message was from our Blessed Mother today. I was so happy to explain to them that it was "to love and to give." In Italian, that is "amare and donare." They were happy to hear the message. I asked them if they had heard the lady screaming today. The women said they heard and saw the lady. The lady was screaming, vomiting, and crawling on the floor. Two priests then came and did an exorcism, and the lady was able to calm down. I then asked if they had seen the apparition of our Blessed Mother. One of them said that she saw our Blessed Mother in the sky with her blue dress with both hands facing down. By hearing this, I felt the Blessed Mother's presence even though I did not see Mary.

I was very happy and had a very good confession. Through reconciliation, we get graces from God that I mentioned before from Saint Faustina's diary! I want to briefly explain about the confession and reconciliation with God and our neighbor (parents, siblings, spouses, children, and whomever we meet in our daily life). At each moment, we need to be in union with GOD and his teaching; this information we can obtain from the BIBLE and the teaching of the Catholic Church. Sometimes we see people that are nice, but their heart is far away from God and his teachings. In this case, God, who sees our heart, is telling us to repent and come back to him. This is the first commandment of GOD—to love your GOD with all your heart and mind and to love your neighbor as yourself, even if that is your enemy.

Jesus is teaching us to love like he did and to forgive like he did. During the time of confession, you only see yourself and the priest, but in each confessional room, Jesus is present invisibly because Jesus is GOD AND HE is omnipotent. Jesus gives the authority to his disciples to absolve all sins from their people. In the Gospel of Saint John 20:19–23 (GNT) says,

> It was late that Sunday evening, and the disciples were gathered together behind locked doors, because they were afraid of the Jewish authorities. Then Jesus came and stood among them. "Peace be with you," he said. After saying this, he showed them his hands and his side. The disciples were filled with joy at seeing the Lord. Jesus said to them again, "Peace be with you. As the Father sent me, so I send you." Then he breathed on them and said, "Receive the Holy Spirit. If you forgive people's sins, they are forgiven; if you do not forgive them, they are not forgiven."

Jesus is giving authority and teaching the priests, bishops, cardinals, and the pope to forgive sins. The Catholic Church is the continuation of Christ, and the Holy Spirit is leading the Church. The Holy Spirit is teaching us the importance of confessing our sins to the priest and teaches us about confession in Saint John's first letter in chapter 1, verses 7 to 10 (GNT).

> But if we live in the light—just as he is in the light—then we have fellowship with one another, and the blood of Jesus, his Son, purifies us from every sin. If we say that we have no sin, we deceive ourselves, and there is no truth in us. But if we confess our sins to God, he will keep his promise and do what is right: he will forgive us our sins and purify us from all our wrongdoing. If we say that we have not sinned, we make a liar out of God, and his word is not in us.

When humans choose to sin, we are satisfying our body and we sin against GOD too! This Saint Paul teaches us in Romans 1:18–25 and 28–32. The best way to get rid of sin is to repent and stay away from all wrongdoing. We must come back to our loving God with full-hearted love toward GOD by sincere repentance from our heart, who is waiting for our return! As God's children, we must believe and be obedient to his Word. As it is written, we should believe in the gospel and repent. In the Gospel of Saint Mark 1:15 (GNT), Jesus is teaching everyone in the world: "'The right time has come,' he said, 'and the Kingdom of God is near! Turn away from your sins and believe the Good News!'"

The next day, my cousin and I decided to recite the rosary in the early morning around 3:30 a.m. near the church. While we were praying the rosary, about three to four dogs ran up to us and started to bark. One of the dogs was even pulling my cousin's shawl that she was wearing. We did not see anyone nearby to call for help. At first, we were afraid, but then all of a sudden, we got the courage and started to pray loudly. As we were praising God, the dogs began to calm down after a few minutes. They even sat nearby while we did the prayer. That was a great experience that we encountered with our Blessed Mother's help.

*Rosa Mystica*

The heavenly Father chose the Blessed Mother as his daughter to help save mankind by being the mother of God. Marian apparitions are when Mary appears in different parts of the world, and when she comes to a particular place, she adopts the culture of that place to be united with that area and the people. For example, when she came to Velankanni in Madras, India, I heard and saw all the pictures and statues of Mary wearing a saree, which is the traditional Indian dress.

Montichiari, Italy, is a small place where Rosa Mystica can be found. It was here that our Blessed Mother appeared to a nurse named Pierina Gilli, a humble Italian woman. My husband and I joined a spiritual pilgrimage group going to Rosa Mystica in October 2019.

We took a bus from Switzerland to Italy that took six hours. On the way, we did the Rosary and prayed the prayer of seven sorrows of our Blessed Mother. On our journey, we were blessed with one bishop and three priests to guide us spiritually.

When we reached the place, we were doing a Rosary precession, and some of the group members smelled a sweet fragrance, which was a sign that our Blessed Mother was present. We were there for two days, and on one of those days, I, along with a few other people, completed the consecration to the immaculate heart of Mary. This is a special prayer to be recited thirty-three days consecutively to Jesus through Mary. On one of the days, we attended a charismatic retreat that was led by a charismatic preacher, who is a priest and joined us from Kerala. He told everyone to close their eyes and pray for a gift from our Blessed Mother. He then said that each one of us would get what we asked for.

I really wanted to get a small Rosa Mystica statue of our Blessed Mother. And I told the Blessed Mother the specific instruction about the face and the same statue that I need because I see that same statue in my cousin's house, and also many people bring the same small statues from their home to get blessed. (It looks so beautiful and looks alive!) Because this is the same place our Blessed Mother appeared in the name of *Rosa Mystica*, I asked for that gift and did not tell anyone, not even my husband. I knew in my heart that it would be very difficult to get that gift because I already have many statues of our Blessed Mother. But I trusted her intervention!

I asked my husband if he was going to buy any statues, and he said that he did not see any statue that he liked, and we left Italy the next day and we traveled back to Switzerland to my cousin's home where we were staying. Then the next day, we got back home to the USA. While I was unpacking, I found something hard wrapped very carefully with a cloth and I was so eager to open it! And when I opened it to see, I couldn't believe my eyes—the beautiful statue of Rosa Mystica, the exact gift I asked our Blessed Mother!

This is the picture of the gift.

At first, I thought that my cousin bought it for me, but when I asked my husband about it, he said that he bought it but kept it a secret so he could surprise me. I was so happy and thanked our Blessed Mother, Jesus, and my beloved husband too!

Jesus gave all the authority of heaven to his mother to be the distributor of graces. Our prayers are answered very fast through our Blessed Mother. Our Blessed Mother is the Queen of heaven and earth and also to all the angels and saints. Wherever our Blessed Mother appeared, she gave a message to the people about the importance of repentance, prayer, fasting, and penance. Our heavenly Father does not want a single soul to be lost. That is why our Blessed Mother is still appearing in Medjugorje and other places, giving the message to the people to pray more at this present time.

In the Gospel of Saint JOHN 15:16 (NABRE) stated, "It was not you who chose me, but I who chose you and appointed you to go and bear fruit that will remain, so that whatever you ask the Father in my name he may give you."

When my daughter, Navya, was in the twelfth grade, she came and asked me, "Mom do you want to recite the fifty-four-day Rosary novena with me?" I asked her what it was with much enthusiasm, and she explained that we will do the Rosary for fifty-four days. In the first twenty-seven days, we can request as many petitions as we want to our Blessed Mother, and the last twenty-seven days, we do not ask for anything but we just do thanksgiving. This was the first time I was hearing about this special Rosary prayer in my life.

I was thinking about how my daughter knew about all these things. I did not teach this to her, but then I realized that the Holy Spirit is teaching all these spiritual encounters to people! Then my daughter and I did this fifty-four-day Rosary novena. And on the fifty-fourth-day, something unthinkable happened. I remember that day because the next day was supposed to be my daughter's high school graduation. That morning, we went to the daily Holy Mass. My daughter said she needed the car to go to a friend's house. I gave her the keys, and after about thirty minutes, I got a call from my husband who said that our daughter got into a car accident.

When I reached the accident site, I could not believe my eyes. My daughter was sitting and talking to the other driver in a friendly manner. And she did not even have a small scratch on her body. The other driver was perfectly fine as well. My daughter's car had a lot of damage, but the other car only had one headlight broken. The bumper on my daughter's car was broken and had fallen off. My daughter was miraculously saved from a serious accident. My daughter was wearing her miraculous medal chain on her neck. During our Lady's visit to Catherine Laboure on November 27, 1830, she said the following about the medal, "All who wear it will receive great graces, they should wear it around the neck. Graces will abound for persons who wear it with confidence." She also said, "I protect all those who wear my medal around their neck."

I know for sure that our Blessed Mother protected my daughter that day. I have read many testimonies about people who wore the medal and did not get hurt when they got into an accident. It is said that those who wear the medal with faith will not die in an accident. My husband and I got into a serious car accident in the winter of

2021. We both got our lives back with God's grace, the power of the Word of God, Psalm 91, and Saint Michael's prayer. We both were wearing the miraculous medal around our neck. Now, my daughter (Navya) is going to tell how the Blessed Mother intervened in her most desperate moments, in her own words.

*My Daughter's Testimony*

My faith in God was never personal until eleventh grade when I was bullied by a longtime friend and I became very depressed. I started to pray not because I had a deep faith but because I did not know where else to turn. I started the fifty-four-day Rosary novena, asking God for this friend to be nice to me again. During this time, I asked God to speak to me and randomly opened the Bible to "The Agony in the Garden." This verse pierced my heart: "My Father, if it is possible, let this cup pass from me, yet not as I will but as you will" (Matthew 26:39 NABRE). I felt like Jesus was really speaking to me while reading this, and I felt like he changed my perspective on how to pray through this verse. This was my initial personal encounter with Jesus, and it opened my heart. Although the friend continued to bully me, I slowly became myself again with new spiritual insight. Life has never been the same since then.

The day before my high school graduation, I caused a car accident. At the end of the same summer, I was volunteering in an ambulance that was involved in a accident. I am so thankful God miraculously protected all people involved in both motor vehicle accidents, and I know Mother Mary also had a role in protecting me.

I walked away from that summer believing God has a plan for my life.

I am thankful for my dearest loving Jesus, who is my everything, especially my hero. He is the beginning and the end and He calls my daughter as his own. Sometimes my daughter gives me counsel, and I know that it is guided by the Holy Spirit. My daughter had more insight than me, and I listen to her, and she always tells me, "Jesus is talking through me." Sometimes we argue, but at the end of the day, we realize we both made mistakes. And then the only solution is to say sorry before bedtime, and then we do a short prayer together and laugh it off. How silly we were! Sometimes I do not admit my mistakes, and my daughter teaches me and helps me realize things. I know that sometimes it is my fault. Because of my lack of humility, I did not want to admit the truth. But I am happy that I am realizing all of this and getting to know Christ's love and mercy and the truth about the devil's trap!

At this moment, I would like to share with you my sister's testimony about how the devil attacks us in our daily lives. My sister, Mary Chechy, told me that even though she is in union with God the Father and Jesus, she was not able to recite the Rosary. She was going through emotional and physical suffering. During family prayer, her husband will pray the Rosary, but she could not recite it. She was always sleepy and did not give the Blessed Mother an important role in her life and her spiritual journey.

But then she attended an inner healing charismatic retreat, and afterward, she was able to adopt the Blessed Mother as her own mother. She was able to recite the Rosary without any difficulties. She even said that when she is cooking, she will recite the Hail Mary and she is at peace even though she is going through a difficult time in her life. Now her work is prayer, and she gives Jesus the first priority. She also intercedes for people who are in need. This is what Jesus is asking from each of us. In all of our physical and spiritual needs, our Blessed Mother is interceding to her Son Jesus and, with the Holy Spirit, is guiding us to grow in our spiritual journey.

"Bear one another's burdens, and so you will fulfill the law of Christ" (Galatians 6:2 NABRE).

O sinner be not discouraged but have recourse to Mary in all your necessities. Call her to your assistance, for such is the divine Will that she should help in every kind of necessity.
—Saint Basil

# Chapter 11

## LOVE AND MERCY

Jesus said to Saint Faustina in diary no. 1273,

> My daughter, do you think you have written enough about My mercy? What you have written is but a drop compared to the ocean. I am love and mercy itself. There is no misery that could be a match for My mercy, and neither will misery exhaust it because as it is being granted— it increases. The soul that trusts in My mercy is most fortunate because I Myself take care of it.

Psalm 145:8 (GNT) says, "The Lord is loving and merciful, slow to become angry and full of constant Love." Yes, this is true. We can see GOD's mercy and love throughout the Bible and also when we study the lives of the Israelites. Throughout their history, the Israelites chose not to listen to God. Despite this, God's love and mercy still prevailed. He sent His people multiple prophets who taught the Israelites how to live peacefully and in harmony. The Israelites continued to live in disobedience, and yet God's mercy still poured out to them. God then sent His only Son who came to the world to save everyone. This can be seen in 1 John 4:9–10 (GNT), which says, "And God showed his love for us by sending his only Son into the world, so that we might have life through him. This is what love is: it is not that we have loved God, but that he loved us and sent his Son to be the means by which our sins are forgiven."

In 1 Corinthians 13:1–13, it says that the Holy Spirit is teaching us about the definition of love. Love is the definition of who Jesus is, and as followers of Jesus, we must love others like Jesus did. In this chapter, I would like to say that God is asking us to do two things: we must show love and mercy toward everyone. The best example of this is Jesus. He willingly sacrificed Himself so that all of the people in the world may receive salvation: the living, the dead, and those yet to be born. This is seen in Acts 4:10–12 (NABRE), which says,

> Then all of you and all the people of Israel should know that it was in the name of Jesus Christ the Nazorean whom you crucified, whom God raised from the dead; in his name this man stands before you healed. He is 'the stone rejected by you, the builders, which has become the cornerstone.' There is no salvation through anyone else, nor is there any other name under heaven given to the human race by which we are to be saved.

It is also seen again in Philippians 2:6–11 (NABRE),

> Who, though he was in the form of God, did not regard equality with God something to be grasped. Rather, he emptied himself, taking the form of a slave, coming in human likeness; and found human in appearance, he humbled himself, becoming obedient to death, even death on a cross. Because of this, God greatly exalted him and bestowed on him the name that is above every name, that at the name of Jesus every knee should bend, of those in heaven and on earth and under the earth, and every tongue confess that

Jesus Christ is the Lord, to the glory of God the
Father.

It is very clear that God showed his love to the world through
his son Jesus, who died on the cross by carrying our sins.

In the present time, God is showing his mercy to his children
by sending his beloved daughter Mary to different parts of the world.
There are many apparitions and private revelations happening all
over the world to this day. I would now like to focus on one private
revelation that Jesus revealed to his beloved daughter and his secretary, Saint Faustina, a Polish nun who lived only thirty-three years in
this world (1905–1938). Saint Faustina had a vision of Jesus Christ
who asked her to write everything that he told her in vision and in
person. She was also known as the secretary of Jesus, and the apostles
of Divine Mercy were chosen by Jesus himself to convey his message
of love and mercy to all people in the world to prepare them for his
second coming!

I did not know what message to write from Saint Faustina's
diary, so I prayerfully took the diary and asked Jesus, "What would
you like me to write about your messages from the diary of Saint
Faustina?" I closed my eyes, opened the book, and read the first passage that caught my eye. It was diary no. 1074 from the third para-
graph, which read, **"Tell (all people), My daughter, that I am love
and mercy itself. When a soul approaches Me with trust, I fill it
with such an abundance of graces that it cannot contain them
within itself but radiates them to other souls."**

Diary no. 1075 reads,

> **Souls who spread the honor of My
> mercy I shield through their entire lives as a
> tender mother her infant, and at the hour of
> death I will not be a judge for them but the
> Merciful Savior. At that last hour, a soul has
> nothing with which to defend itself expect My
> mercy. Happy is the soul that during its life-**

time immersed itself in the fountain of mercy because justice will have no hold on it.

Diary no. 1076, meanwhile, also reads,

**Write this: Everything that exists is enclosed in the bowels of My mercy, more deeply than an infant in its mother's womb. How painfully distrust of My goodness wounds Me! Sins of distrust wound Me most painfully.**

I first read these passages by opening the diary and reading the first entries that caught my eye. I was amazed at how Jesus was carefully guiding me to these passages. I know that he did this so I could talk about his mercy and let others come to know about it too. Jesus pours his love and mercy to the whole world, but so many people are unaware of this. I, too, was unaware, but in 2011, Jesus caught me like one of his own disciples. And now I try to tell others of Jesus's mercy. I had Saint Faustina's diary for a few years, but I never read it. However, when I started writing this book, I got the inspiration to look up these quotes from the diary. In fact, this is the first time I opened the diary to read it.

If anyone is looking for peace in their hearts and minds, immerse yourself in the sacred heart of Jesus. There may be days where we feel lonely even though we have all our loved ones around us. We may not know what to do or whom to turn to. Jesus told Saint Faustina in diary no. 300, **"Mankind will not have peace until it turns with trust to My mercy. Oh, how much I am hurt by a soul's distrust! Such a soul professes that I am holy and just but does not believe that I am mercy and does not trust in My goodness. Even the devils glorify My justice but do not believe in My goodness. My heart rejoices in this title of mercy."** Diary no. 301 reads, **"Proclaim that mercy is the greatest attribute of GOD. All the works of My hands are crowned with mercy."**

At that moment, think about only one person who is our best friend in the world. That best friend is JESUS, whom we can trust with our life; not anyone but Jesus is the only living GOD who is waiting for your call at any time, day or night, twenty-four hours, watching you and me, and pause one minute and call on Jesus's mobile phone. If you don't know the number, let me tell you, it's JEREMIAH 33:3 (GNT), "Call to me, and I will answer you; I will tell you wonderful and marvelous things that you know nothing about."

Yes, my dearest friends, we can rely on Jesus. That I am writing this from my own experiences when I went through the struggles, I experienced all that I have mentioned above. When I held Jesus tightly in my heart, I saw his love pouring on me. That love, no man can give it to you, even your beloved spouse, children, or whoever you may choose to have a close relationship with. Jesus is our only true friend in this world.

It's written in Philippians 4:13 (GNT), "I have the strength to face all conditions by the power that Christ gives me." Also, verse 19 (GNT) teaches us, "And with all his abundant wealth through Christ Jesus, my God will supply all your needs." Yes, it's the truth that when we are in Jesus's presence and constantly seeking him, we can find him. No, he will find us. He is very near to each and every one. To see him, we need to open our minds and open our inner eyes. He is the hidden treasure and he is the good shepherd looking after his sheep. For that reason, why do we need to worry and get anxious about anything? Just abandon ourselves to his sacred heart.

In JOEL 2:12–13 (GNT), it says,

> "But even now," says the Lord, "repent sincerely and return to me with fasting and weeping and mourning. Let your broken heart show your sorrow; tearing your clothes is not enough." Come back to the Lord your God. He is kind and full of mercy; he is patient and keeps his promise; he is always ready to forgive and not punish.

We must give all our brokenness and weakness and anything that is hurting us to our Lord, who is compassionate and slow in anger, rich in mercy and love, and will purify all of our weakness and our brokenness. The heart of Jesus pours out love and mercy toward all who are waiting on Jesus and opening their hearts for Jesus to enter. Jesus says this in Psalm 34:8 (GNT), "Find out for yourself how good the Lord is. Happy are those who find safety with him." Also, in Revelation 3:20–22 (GNT), Jesus is telling everyone in the world,

> Listen! I stand at the door and knock; if any hear my voice and open the door, I will come into their house and eat with them, and they will eat with me. To those who win the victory I will give the right to sit beside me on my throne, just as I have been victorious and now sit by my Father on his throne. If you have ears, then, listen to what the Spirit says to the churches!

A couple of months ago, I was talking to one of my friends about the book that I am writing. We were discussing our personal encounter with Jesus and how it helped our spiritual journey. She was telling me how she was living worldly and was going through some physical and emotional struggles. She told me that her mom, who is a person of prayer, told her to get prayer from a spiritual counselor, who is a layperson very close to Jesus, and spend hours in Eucharistic adoration. She was not able to see the person because he was in Kerala, a state in India, but she called him over the phone. On the phone, this spiritual counselor told her, "I am seeing a vision of Jesus knocking at your heart, and you are not opening the door for him and that the Blessed Mother is also crying."

The counselor also told her to remove some items from the house, go for a good confession, read the Bible daily, and attend a stay-in retreat. This type of retreat gives you an opportunity to be detached from the world; concentrate on prayer; listen to the Word of God; and attend the daily Holy Mass, Eucharistic adoration, and confession. My friend knew what she had to remove from the house and followed the spiritual counselor's instructions. She went for a stay-in retreat with a focus on fasting where she was only allowed to drink water on those three days, and she even had a great confession.

During these retreats, the preacher who is led by the Holy Spirit taught us how to do a good confession and pray. They guided us through praise and worship and helped us to receive spiritual nourishment. In fact, my friend told me how this retreat changed her life and helped her get closer to Jesus. She even got a personal encounter with Jesus!

She told me this was the first time that she was attending a fasting retreat. When there is fasting; we are doing sacrifices and giving up food that itself gets special blessings. (But in all other retreats, there will be food provided, and it is up to us if we want to fast or not.) She told me that the true full confession helped her to be free from the bondages and what was affecting her, and she got a peace that no one could give her. Jesus is the only one who can give this peace because He *is* that peace. When Jesus comes to our hearts, truly, we are in peace with Jesus and everyone that we meet. Then it is easy for us to forgive like Jesus did and love like Jesus did. Jesus is the Prince of peace.

What is a good confession? By now, you may be thinking, is there a good confession and a regular confession? Of course, there are two types. Some people may not know how to do a good confession from their hearts. I can tell you from my experience that I did not know how to do a good confession until I learned how to do a good confession from the many retreats I attended and from the Holy Spirit's inspirations. To prepare for a good confession, we must first sit in the presence of the Lord in silence with a Bible, paper, and pen, but do not write anything yet.

After, we must pray to the Holy Spirit and pray with the intercession of our Blessed Mother. Prayerfully take a passage from the Bible and read it. Then ask the Holy Spirit to reveal our sins. Sometimes, we even forgot what we did wrong to others, but the Holy Spirit will remind us and help us remember the sins we forgot. Now take the paper and pen and start to write; you don't even have to think, it comes to your mind fluently.

The next step is to thank the Holy Spirit and acknowledge him for helping you. Then you can go to the confession with that paper whenever the next available time for confession, or you can make an appointment to do the confession from your local parish or any priest who is available to hear your confession appointed by Jesus. It is better not to delay the confession. The prayer that I do before the confession is the prayer our Blessed Mother taught to Fr. Stefano Gobbi (March 22, 1930–June 29, 2011), "Come, Holy Spirit, come by means of the powerful intercession of the immaculate heart of Mary, your well-beloved spouse." I encourage you to pray this prayer and the Hail Mary prayer three times. We must also pray for the priest who hears our confession.

It is a beautiful prayer. Anytime we need help from the Holy Spirit, we can pray this prayer. It is very powerful when we do it in faith. Our every action depends on our faith. I have mentioned in the previous chapter about the benefits of confession. In Sirach 2:11 (NABRE), it teaches us, "For the Lord is compassionate and merciful; forgives sins and saves in time of trouble."

Let us go back to Jesus's message in the diary no. 1074 and 1075. This shows how much Jesus wants us to return to him. It is important that we, God's chosen ones, proclaim his mercy to the world. Many people are still unaware of God's mercy. Jesus told Saint Faustina this in diary no. 1146.

> **[Let] the greatest sinners place their trust in my mercy. They have the right before others to trust in the abyss of My mercy. My daughter, write about My mercy toward tormented souls. Souls that make an appeal to My mercy delight Me. To such souls I grant even more graces than they ask. I cannot punish even the greatest sinner if he makes an appeal to My compassion, but on the contrary, I justify him in My unfathomable and inscrutable**

**mercy. Write: before I come as a just Judge, I first open wide the door of My mercy. He who refuses to pass through the door of My mercy must pass through the door of my justice.**

Here, Jesus is talking about HIS second coming as a judge! So this is the hour of mercy.

The hour of mercy is now. Since no one knows when JESUS will return from heaven during the second coming, it is our responsibility to come to JESUS's merciful heart. We must take refuge in His sacred heart; God the Father does not want any soul to be lost in the eternal fire at the end! Jesus's passion and death were only for our salvation, so when we sin, we are hurting Jesus. Let's love Jesus and stop our sinful ways. We must love everyone we meet and rely upon Jesus's mercy. In fact, Jesus told Saint Faustina in diary no. 327 about the picture of the Divine Mercy: **"I am offering people a vessel with which they are to keep coming for graces to the fountain of mercy. That vessel is this image with the signature: Jesus, I trust in You."** This is the Divine Mercy Jesus.

This is my special statue of Divine Mercy. I got it for my birthday.

This is the original Divine Mercy image.

Jesus taught the Divine Mercy chaplet prayer to be recited at 3:00 p.m. to remember his passion and death. We must pray the Divine Mercy chaplet at 3:00 p.m. for the whole world. Diary no. 848 quotes Saint Faustina hearing the voice of Christ saying,

> **While I was saying the chaplet, I heard a voice which said, "Oh, what great graces I will grant to souls who say this chaplet; the very depths of My tender mercy are stirred for the sake of those who say the chaplet. Write down these words, My daughter. Speak to the world about My mercy and let all mankind recognize My unfathomable mercy. It is a sign for the end-times. After it will come (230) the day of justice. While there is still time, let them have recourse to the fount of My mercy; let them**

**profit from the blood and water which gushed
forth for them.**

Saint Faustina also had a vision of heaven, hell, and purgatory. What she described about heaven is what Saint Paul says in 1 Corinthians 2:9–10 (NABRE): "But as it is written: 'What eye has not seen, and ear has not heard, and what has not entered the human heart, what God has prepared for those who love him,' this God has revealed to us through the Spirit. For the Spirit scrutinizes everything, even the depths of God."

In diary no. 741 of Saint Maria Faustina Kowalska, she writes,

**I, Sister Faustina, by the order of God,
have visited the abysses of hell so that I might
tell souls about it and testify to its existence. I
cannot speak about it now, but I have received
a command from God to leave it in writing.
The devils were full of hatred for me, but they
had to obey me at the command of God. What
I have written is but a pale shadow of the
things I saw. But I noticed one thing: most of
the souls there are those who disbelieved that
there is a hell.**

In the Gospel, Jesus has taught us about the people who are ignorant of other people's needs and will be judged accordingly to their deeds. Many people do not want to believe that there is hell. This is very dangerous for the soul because it is the devil's trap. Some people may think that it is okay to live in darkness and that God will be merciful and so they will be saved. This is not the way. Throughout the Bible, from Genesis to Revelation, the Holy Spirit is teaching us to trust in the Lord and to repent from wrongdoing/sin and come back to God. God is merciful, and his love is forever enduring and constantly forgiving our sins when we repent from our heart. It is written in ISAIAH 66:2 (GNT), "I myself created the whole universe!

I am pleased with those who are humble and repentant, who fear me and obey me."

I started to pray more after I got the healing from cancer. However, there were two times when I fell from just walking. In the first incident, I was walking very slowly in the basement, and there was no water on the floor, but then suddenly, I was turned in such a way that I hit my right chest on the railing of the staircase. It felt like someone was pushing me into the railing, and I got severe pain in my surgical site. In the second incident, the same thing happened, but this time, I fell to the floor. With God's grace, nothing happened. I only had some pain. I did not think much of these incidents but was pondering in my heart about what happened.

Then one day, while I was sleeping, I felt as if someone was choking me and I was unable to breathe. I could feel someone's hand around my neck. I suddenly woke up and called Jesus's name and I felt free and was able to breathe. I then understood that it was my enemy, the devil, that was doing all these things. After this incident, I started to wear the Blessed Mother brown scapular with the Benedictine cross and the miraculous medal. With God's grace, I never got that kind of attack again. That was an eye-opening incident for me to pray more and trust in our Lord's mercy and to also seek the importance of the intercession prayer with our Blessed Mother by doing the Rosary daily, as well as keeping the whole world consecrated to the immaculate heart of Mary.

If you ask me if I have heard Jesus's voice, the answer is yes. With God's grace, I have heard it two times when I was sleeping. The first time was around 2:45 p.m. I heard my name being called, "LILLY," out loud and I woke up suddenly and said, "Yes." But I did not see anyone. The second time was around 2:50 a.m., and again, I heard, "LILLY," said out loud. I thought it was my husband, so I called his name, "Johneychaya," but when I looked at him, I saw that he was in deep sleep. However, I stayed awake at both times and did the Divine Mercy chaplet for all the people in the world at 3:00 p.m. and 3:00 a.m. I knew Jesus was waking me up to do the Divine Mercy chaplet for the world.

I want to tell a testimony about how my family experienced love and mercy from Jesus, the King of mercy. As I mentioned before, I used to watch Shalom TV on a daily basis. One day, I was enthusiastically listening to a talk given by a priest about the reverence we ought to give while reciting the Divine Mercy chaplet. He said to place a white cloth on the table, place a cross or a Divine Mercy image and a candle, and then pray the Divine Mercy chaplet *while fully entrusting ourselves and intentions to Jesus's merciful heart*. I began to pray the chaplet in this way. One summer day in 2017 at 3:00 p.m., the very first time I placed a white cloth on the table with the Divine Mercy statue and candle, a miracle happened.

My daughter Nancy was coming home from New Jersey around that time, and she called us at 4:00 p.m., saying she got into an accident on the highway. With God's grace, there were no injuries on anyone, just minor damage on our Honda Civic. When I took my daughter to the doctor, the doctor had said it was really a miracle that she walked away without any injuries. I knew in my heart Jesus saved her from a potentially dangerous accident, and I am ever grateful to my king and master, Jesus Christ, for keeping her and all others safe.

Throughout my life, I have seen God's mercy being poured out to my family. When we are faithful to God, he is also faithful to us. In Luke 1:50 (GNT), it teaches us, "From one generation to another he shows mercy to those who honor him," and Psalm 103:1–8 also teaches us about God's mercy. One night, before I went to bed, my mind was a little disturbed and restless. I was not able to sleep. Usually, when this happens, I pray the Hail Mary or simply call Jesus's name.

I woke up the next morning by hearing this Word of God, "Ephesians 2:14." I did not hear the passage, just that word and chapter and verse number. I did not know what the verse was, and so I opened the Bible to Ephesians 2:14 (GNT), and it states, "For Christ himself has brought us peace by making Jews and Gentiles one people, with his own body he broke down the wall that separated them and kept them enemies." This Word of God amazed me. I had not read this passage before, and it was the first time I had seen this Word of GOD! After reading this, I felt so much peace in my mind.

Now I know for sure that Jesus knows everything about you and me, even if you do not know him.

I want to retell a story I heard in a sermon that moved me. There once was a king who invited his people to the palace. He exclaimed, "Within the hour, whatever you touch in the palace is yours." Many people touched many material items, but one child came and touched the king. The king was moved and took the child in as his own, resulting in the child inheriting all of the material goods the king had. In the same way, our heavenly Father is waiting for us to go to him and touch him, to open our hearts to him, and to invite him into our lives. God is available to all; Jesus came for this very reason, to give us himself. Sometimes we go to God for material things and blessings, and this is good. He is eager to bless us. What is better and the best is receiving Jesus into our lives. In this way of accepting the Lord, all material things and blessings will follow, along with joy, love, and our deepest desires will be fulfilled. We are all children of God, but when we choose to accept and live in this identity, we will experience being the son or daughter of a king. In the Gospel of Saint John 6:35 (NABRE) says, "Jesus said to them, 'I am the bread of life; whoever comes to me will never hunger, and whoever believes in me will never thirst.'"

He is waiting every morning for us to come and see him at the blessed sacraments. Are we aware of this? Matthew 13:44 (GNT) says, "The Kingdom of heaven is like this. A man happens to find a treasure hidden in a field. He covers it up again, and is so happy that he goes and sells everything he has, and then goes back and buys that field." Jesus is teaching us to do the same, just like the man that found the treasure hidden in the field. That treasure is Jesus himself.

I want to tell you how the front and back cover designs of this book came about. I can honestly say that the Holy Spirit helped me with each step of the process of writing this book and making the design for the cover picture of this book, front and back. And I must acknowledge the Holy Spirit for his help, and all glory is given to the HOLY TRINITY!

When I started writing the book, I did not have any idea of what to put on the covers. I thought that I could take any picture from the internet, but my son-in-law, Joe, told me that there might be a copyright issue. After a few days, I was talking with my sister, Regi, who said that our cousin brother, Shaji, from India, drew beautifully. And so I contacted him and gave him specific instructions. He then gave the instructions to his brother Nixon's daughter, Nicole. She drew both pictures very beautifully. On the front cover, she drew a picture of Jesus holding a baby, who is my first granddaughter, Cecelia. And on the back cover, it is me in the field from Matthew 13:44. When Nicole drew the back cover of this book, I liked it at first. When I showed my son, he said the picture looked like Jesus in white clothing. So I decided to tell Nicole to make the dress blue with lily flowers, and she did. When I was attending a one-day retreat from the UK via Zoom, I was able to participate in a one-on-one spiritual sharing. I had requested prayers for the book I was writing. The brother I spoke with had a vision of many lily flowers on top of a book. Then he asked me what that was, and I explained to him about the book cover. I was so happy I got confirmation that Jesus liked the cover design of my book, and I thanked God.

When the front cover was already drawn with so many bright colors, one of the priests saw the cover and suggested to make it more natural, if possible. I had no idea how to go about this, so I started to pray to the Holy Spirit, who is the chief counselor of everything—physical, spiritual, and mental. After that, I got an image in my mind of a garden with natural elements, and I knew this was for the front cover. Everything in nature glorifies God, who created the universe. I proceeded to give specific instructions to my niece Nicole, who drew everything as I explained. I thank God for Nicole; she has helped me so much.

I want to especially acknowledge the Holy Spirit, who is my chief counselor for everything I do. My dearest Holy Spirit, my helper, my counselor, and the dearest in my heart, I thank you and love you for helping me throughout the phase of writing this book and for giving me counsel, design, and wisdom to complete this book. I would like to acknowledge and give glory and honor to Jesus, who gave me the title of this book. And I would like to thank Abba

Father for helping me to accomplish the writing about my spiritual and physical journey.

Ten years ago, while I was attending the Holy Mass, the gospel reading was from Matthew 13. During the reading, verse 44 came into my heart, but as soon as the Holy Mass concluded, I forgot about this Word. This was the first Word of God that touched my heart. But unfortunately, the devil stole it from my heart before it could bear fruit. As Jesus taught us in Mark 4:14–15 (GNT), "The sower sows God's message. Some people are like the seeds that fall along the path; as soon as they hear the message, Satan comes and takes it away." I was like the seed that was at the roadside for ten years after I heard the Word of God. But with Jesus's infinite mercy, I was able to come back to Jesus's heart where I belong. In the First Letter of John 4:4 (GNT) says, "But you belong to God, my children, and have defeated the false prophets, because the Spirit who is in you is more powerful than the spirit in those who belong to the world."

The Holy Spirit is teaching us that Jesus's spirit is inside us and is greater than the spirit who is of the world, which is the enemy, the devil. Remember, we only have one enemy. But God is greater than the enemy, and so there is no reason to fear. Like it says in Romans 8:31 (GNT), "If God is for us, who can be against us?"

I am taking this time to acknowledge my love for Jesus. But it is he who loved me first, as it is written in the First Letter of Saint John 4:19–21 (GNT), "We love because God first loved us. If we say we love God, but hate others, we are liars. For we cannot love God, whom we have not seen, if we do not love others, whom we have seen. The command that Christ has given us is this: whoever loves God must love others also."

Jesus loves me as a precious jewel. Through this book, which is titled *My Jesus, My Hero* that Jesus himself gave to me, I am an instrument of his will. Jesus, I know that my writings are not great, but this is your book, you are the *author*. Please give your wisdom to all those who read this book to know you personally. All the wisdom is hidden in you, Jesus, as it is written in Colossians 2:3 (GNT), "He is the key that opens all the hidden treasures of God's wisdom and knowledge."

May the truth about JESUS be revealed to each person who is reading this book with the grace of the HOLY SPIRIT. I pray to you, Lord Jesus, that your blessing and graces will be poured out to all the readers and that your Holy Spirit will be sent to each one of them from your mighty power.

Lord Jesus, I bring to you all of the people that are going through struggles, including those feeling hopeless, in pain, depressed, sick, oppressed, imprisoned, and any other kind of struggles, as well as those who do not know you. I pray that they will be able to see the light coming into their hearts. That light is you, Jesus. Please help them find you in their hearts. I humbly request that you reveal yourself to all of the people that do not know you personally, and for those that do know you, please hold them with your mighty wounded hands and allow them to have a personal relationship with you.

Lord Jesus, please heal all the people that call upon your name, Abba Father. Please hear them from heaven and heal them because, Abba Father, you made heaven and earth and everything in it. Nothing is impossible with you. As it is written in Luke 1:37 (GNT), "For there is nothing that God cannot do." This I pray in Jesus's name. Amen.

# Conclusion

I would like to conclude this book with what Jesus has taught us to do: have responsibility for each other's well-being, love one another, and be patient, kind, and merciful to one another. We ought to strive for these kinds of virtues every day starting in our own homes and also show the same to our neighbors so that they may come to know of God's love for them. In doing so, we may be able to help others grow in the love of Jesus, which will ultimately benefit them and the entire world. When we are open to knowing Christ, he reveals Himself to us. He helps us to see the truth about ourselves, and therefore, we receive the opportunity to become better versions of ourselves. As Jesus taught us in the Gospel of Saint John 14:21 (GNT), "Those who accept my commandments and obey them are the ones who love me. My Father will love those who love me; I too will love them and reveal myself to them."

Furthermore, it is written in Acts 4:11–12 (GNT) that salvation is only through Jesus who is the true God. It states, "Jesus is the one of whom the scripture says, 'The stone that you the builders despised turned out to be the most important of all.' Salvation is to be found through him alone; in all the world there is no one else whom God has given who can save us."

One of my favorite saints is Catherine of Siena (March 25, 1347–April 29, 1380). She only lived thirty-three years in this world, but before she died, she set the world on fire by following Jesus and showing his love to others. She said, "Be who God meant you to be and you will set the world on fire," and "Start being brave about everything. Drive out darkness and spread light. Don't look at your weaknesses. Realize instead that in Christ crucified you can do everything."

For it is written in 1 Peter 3: 8–12 (GNT),

> To conclude: you must all have the same attitude and the same feelings; love one another, and be kind and humble with one another. Do not pay back evil with evil or cursing with cursing; instead, pay back with a blessing, because a blessing is what God promised to give you when he called you. As the scripture says, If you want to enjoy life and wish to see good times, you must keep from speaking evil and stop telling lies. You must turn away from evil and do good; you must strive for peace with all your heart. For the Lord watches over the righteous and listens to their prayers; but he opposes those who do evil.

My dearest readers, we have been traveling together for a while. Now what else is left to say before we depart? Thank you for taking the time to read about my physical and spiritual journey. I will be praying for all of you. I would like to end with some final takeaways. Jesus is our Lord and Savior, and He died for our salvation. Jesus is knocking at the door of our hearts, and it is our free choice to open the door for Him to enter. May you experience the Good Shepherd's love, hope, faith, joy, peace, and much more. I hope you all experience the love that Jesus wants to pour out onto you.

THE END

# About the Author

Lilly Simon was born and brought up in Kerala, India. She came to the US as a nurse at the age of twenty-two with an intention to find a better life for herself and her loved ones. She worked as a registered nurse at different hospitals and nursing homes for twenty-six years in New York. She is now retired and enjoys spending time participating in daily Holy Mass and visits to the Blessed Sacrament, along with participating in intercessory prayers with various prayer groups. She loves to read spiritual books and travel, especially to visit pilgrimage sites. She loves to cook, and her children enjoy her various traditional Indian dishes. She is a first-time author with the grace of God almighty. She would like to give all glory to the Holy Trinity for this achievement.

Lilly is married to her beloved husband, Johney. She has four children who are all dear to her heart—Noel, Nancy, Navya (Nova, who is in Heaven), daughter-in-law Ashley, son-in-law Joe, and two beloved grandchildren, Cecelia and Leo. She strongly believes that all her blessings are gifts from heaven above. She is loved by her family and friends. She never had a plan to write a book, but as it is written in Jeremiah 29:11 (GNT), "I alone know the plans I have for you, plans to bring you prosperity and not disaster, plans to bring about the future you hope for," and the rest is history.

Printed in the USA
CPSIA information can be obtained
at www.ICGtesting.com
LVHW020301141023
760905LV00005B/29